The Amazing Race

The Amazing Race

WINNING THE TECHNORIVALRY WITH JAPAN

William H. Davidson
University of Virginia

JOHN WILEY & SONS

New York   Chichester   Brisbane   Toronto   Singapore

This publication is designed to provide accurate and
authoritative information in regard to the subject
matter covered. It is sold with the understanding that
the publisher is not engaged in rendering legal, accounting,
or other professional service. If legal advice or other
expert assistance is required, the services of a competent
professional person should be sought. *From a Declaration
of Principles jointly adopted by a Committee of the
American Bar Association and a Committee of Publishers.*

Library of Congress Cataloging in Publication Data:

Davidson, William Harley, 1951–
    The amazing race.

    Includes index.
    1. Computer industry—Japan.   2. Computer industry—
United States.   3. Data transmission equipment industry—
Japan.   4. Data transmission equipment industry—United
States.   5. Competition, International.   I. Title.
HD9696.C63J3135   1984   338.4′70015′0952   83-12353
ISBN 0-471-88711-0

Printed in the United States of America

10 9 8 7 6 5 4 3 2 1

To my wife
Anneke

Preface

The United States is engaged in a two-front war against specialized rivals. It competes with the USSR in the military arena and with Japan and other nations in the industrial arena. The USSR neglects its industrial activities to focus on military efforts; Japan neglects its military to concentrate on industrial endeavors. If the United States is to retain its world leadership in these two arenas, it must dominate those sectors that are critical to success in both. The information technology sector—including computer and communication equipment and services—is vital to both military and industrial leadership.

If the information technology sector continues to grow at its current average annual rate of 15%, it will account for approximately 40% of world industrial value-added by the end of the century. This growth rate is uniquely attractive to companies and nations, and rivals of all possible shapes and sizes will contend to secure positions in this market.

For the Japanese, the information technology sector offers a vehicle to achieve their manifest destiny. Since the Meiji restoration, they have sought a position of leadership, pride, and prestige in the Western world. By gaining preeminence in information technology, they see the opportunity to attain that position. Their fifth-generation computer project is equivalent to the American moon shot, and the country is funneling national resources and energies into information technology with single-minded zeal and dedication. Every aspect of Japanese industrial policy and life will be focused on this effort.

The United States has begun to marshal its resources in response. Massive changes occurring in management philosophies and strategies, in public policies, and in labor and capital markets are stimulated by the need to increase industrial competitiveness, especially in fields related to communications and information technology.

The two countries are engaged in an intense and complex race, for immense stakes. It is, however, very different from the arms race. The world's peoples can benefit only from a reduction in the pace and intensity of the arms race. But the greater the intensity of the information technology race, and the faster the pace of its discoveries, the greater will be the benefits to world society. Competition between the United States and Japan in this sector is a positive and progressive force that will contribute greatly to economic and social progress.

The consequences of the competition will be profound. They will extend far beyond their participants, and all nations will be affected by the outcome of the race. What is less apparent is the extent to which each of us has already been affected. The drive to improve industrial competitiveness has led to fundamental changes in labor and capital markets, in public policies and programs, and in management philosophies and strategies in both countries. The business environment and economic and social conditions in the United States have been irreversibly altered. Companies need to consider how these changes are affecting their prospects. Individuals need to understand their evolving roles as consumers, savers, and workers. These changes have all been stimulated by the success of the Japanese model. To understand their impact in the United States and elsewhere, now and in the future, we must analyze the origins and sources of Japan's success in the industrial arena.

WILLIAM H. DAVIDSON

Charlottesville, Virginia
September 1983

Acknowledgments

This book describes the impact of competition between Japan and the United States on developments in the information technology sector and on broader economic and social conditions in both countries. My thinking on these subjects has been influenced greatly by a number of people. Especially important were Professor Michael Yoshino of Harvard Business School, whose work on the Japanese managerial and business system was path-breaking; Professor John Rosenblum, Dean of the University of Virginia's Colgate Darden School, who was among the first to address the impact of Japanese activities on U.S. industry; and Professor Raymond Vernon of Harvard University's Center for International Studies, who uniquely combines a knowledge of political economy and industrial strategy in the international arena. I was also influenced by the writings of James Abbeglen, Robert Cole, Ronald Dore, Soloman Levine, Chie Nakane, Michael Porter, Edwin Reischauer, and Ezra Vogel, among others.

Frank Parson's unwavering support and encouragement were critical in initiating and continuing my work in this area. I benefited greatly from interaction with Professor Yoshi Tsurumi of Baruch College; Kneale Ashwell, President of Johnson and Johnson (Japan); Lynda Schubert of Schubert Associates; Yoshi Minigeshi; Dick Rutledge; and managers at a number of Japanese organizations, especially Fujitsu, NEC, Hitachi, NTT, Toshiba, Sharp, Matsushita, MITI, and the Bank of Japan.

Other contributions came from Mas Kakutani and Jud Porter, whose assistance in the early phases of this study was most useful; Takao Nakanishi of JETRO, Ed Colby of Apple Computer Company, and Steve Schewe. I also benefited from the comments and thoughts of my colleagues at The Darden School, especially Brandt Allen, Ralph Biggadike, and Bill Harper. Finally, the heroic efforts of Holly Lanigan were essential to the completion of this manuscript, and the assistance of Tammy Stebbins, B. J. Blincoe, Nina Hutchinson, Terri Norcross, and Beth McDermott was greatly appreciated.

W. H. D.

Contents

The Amazing Race

I

The United States and Japan in Retrospect (1959–1979)

1

Origins of Japanese Industrial Strategy

The key to military success is concentration of resources at the critical point and time."
Karl von Clausewitz

The trademark of Japanese industrial activity is an emphasis on old-fashioned price and quality. The combination of low price and superior quality has been fundamental in supporting penetration of world automobile, motorcycle, audio, video, copier, and other industries. Japanese products often enter world markets with prices 25% or more below those of comparable existing products. The first step in understanding the origins of Japanese industrial strategy involves identifying the sources of these price differentials. Do they result from operating efficiencies or public subsidies, or do they merely reflect an alternative approach to pricing and profit making?

Japanese firms have shown an almost universal willingness to accept margins and profits lower than those prevailing in world markets. In the computer industry, for example, the six leading Japanese vendors realized an average profit of 2.7% after tax in 1982. The six largest U.S. producers realized a net profit in excess of 10% of sales. Such profit differentials are a direct result of Japanese pricing strategies.

When reduced prices are used to gain share in existing markets, it is important to distinguish between penetration and predatory pricing. Predatory pricing, widely used in the late nineteenth century in the United States, involves cutting prices below costs in a local market, driving local competitors to bankruptcy, acquiring them, raising prices, and moving on to the next market. The distinction between penetration and predatory pricing is subtle but important. These two strategies differ primarily in terms of degree, intent, and time frame, but other elements of corporate strategy will also differ. Penetration pricing, when complemented by a volume-sensitive production and distribution strategy, can lead to reduction in costs that support long-term reductions in prices. Cost reduction is not a primary goal in a pure predatory pricing strategy. Predatory pricing involves short-term, discrete price cuts intended to eliminate competition and permit higher prices in the long run.

A third type of pricing strategy, discriminatory pricing, entails charging different prices to customers in different markets. This is a common strategy for international companies. Prices for a given product in any market normally reflect the level of market maturity and development. Prices are usually higher in emerging new markets and lower in mature markets. For U.S. companies, this usually translates into higher prices abroad than at home, because the home market is almost always more highly developed than foreign markets. For Japanese companies in the 1950s and 1960s, the reverse was often true. Unfortunately, when discriminatory pricing results in lower prices abroad than at home, a case of dumping exists.

Each of these three types of pricing strategies has been cited as a source of the price differentials for Japanese products. Pricing strategies certainly contribute to observed pricing patterns, but the key issue is efficiency. Is there a cost differential behind Japanese pricing patterns, or are they supported primarily by artificial sources?

One possible source of lower costs is wage rates. Wage rates in Japan averaged 33% of U.S. levels in 1965. Although this wage gap is decreasing rapidly, it was a powerful force in the initial stages of Japanese industrial expansion.

Low wage rates alone will not provide a competitive advantage. Wages are far lower in other Asian nations. Productivity levels must also be compared. Japanese productivity levels, on average, have consistently been below U.S. levels by a factor almost approximating the wage differential. The average Japanese worker in the manufacturing sector produced two-thirds of the average American worker's output in 1975; his wages averaged just over half of the American worker's. Although labor costs remain significantly lower in Japan after adjustment for output rates, net labor costs are converging in the two nations.[1] On the surface, this observation raises questions about the economics underlying Japanese pricing strategies. However, it is important to look beyond average output levels to output rates in individual industries.

In the motorcycle industry, U.S. and European firms produced about 15 motorcycles per worker per year in the early 1970s. Japanese producers turned out more than 200 per worker annually.[2] Even after differences in product size and company vertical integration have been accounted for, Japanese productivity in this industry greatly exceeds that of the United States and Europe. A similar pattern can be found in the automobile industry. Japanese productivity, again adjusted for size and vertical integration, appears to be at least twice as high as productivity in the U.S. auto industry.[3] The steel, audio, and video industries reveal similar productivity ratios. These productivity differentials can only mean that other Japanese industries are woefully inefficient by international standards. Such extremes are a conscious result of national industrial policy.

Karl von Clausewitz was a Prussian military strategist. A general in the Prussian High Command, Clausewitz was a practitioner as well as a theorist. His thoughts on military strategy are contained in a three-volume work entitled *On War*. Although many principles of strategy are discussed in this book, one appears to dominate. The key to military success according to Clausewitz was concentration of resources in critical areas at the critical time. This principle is firmly applied in the Japanese economic system. Financial and human resources are concentrated in critical industries, or target sectors, through a variety of forces and mechanisms. This process accounts for the productivity patterns cited above. Although Japanese industry as a whole is less productive than U.S. industry, in certain sectors it is far more productive. The important question then becomes: Which sectors do the Japanese choose to concentrate in, and why? The answer will provide an understanding of Japanese objectives, motives, and, most important, strategy.

SECTOR SELECTION

The basic issue in sector selection is identifing those sectors which, if pursued successfully, will contribute most to fundamental objectives. The probability of success is a second critical issue. To address the first issue, it is important to understand the basic objectives underlying sector selection decisions. The most fundamental objective for any nation, organization, or individual is survival. When Japan began to rebuild itself in the 1940s and 1950s, survival was the issue. In order to survive, Japan had to import food and fuel. In order to import, it had to export. The export imperative is the most fundamental Japanese objective. What can Japan export? Its only resource is labor; its only export is value added. In order to use its resource most efficiently, Japan must seek to maximize value added per worker. These two basic objectives, to maximize net exports and to maximize value added per worker, have driven all aspects of Japanese activity in the post-war period and they are critical in selecting industrial sectors.

These objectives are helpful in initiating a list of criteria to be used in evaluating alternative industrial sectors. Two criteria immediately emerge. Target sectors should have low import costs per dollar of export revenue. They should also exhibit a cost structure with a high value-added content. These two criteria are highly complementary and adequately reflect the two fundamental objectives. Successful activity in sectors with these characteristics will contribute to basic objectives, but other objectives must also be considered. A full hierarchy of objectives exists beyond survival. The ultimate goals are victory, dominance, and control over one's environment. As basic objectives are met, these goals can be expected to become more important. How can Japan achieve dominance in industrial sectors? What criteria can measure their ability to succeed in different industries? These questions bring us to the heart of Japanese industrial strategy.

ACHIEVING COMPETITIVE ADVANTAGE

One of the most basic principles of strategy is to concentrate resources in sectors the investing entity can dominate. In order to dominate a sector, some source of competitive advantage is required. For Japan, the major source of that competitive advantage has been manufacturing efficiency. Japanese industry has generally attempted to achieve dominance through cost leadership. A single-minded drive to achieve cost leadership has largely determined the nature of Japanese industrial strategy.

Generalizations about industrial strategy are of course

extremely hazardous. Exceptions can always be found. Nonetheless, the record of successful Japanese industries suggests some patterns. First and foremost perhaps is the manufacturing component of industrial strategies. Japanese firms have followed highly similar paths in competing for world automobile, consumer electronics, motorcycle, steel, and other industries. Manufacturing operations tend to be highly automated, capital-intensive, and conducted in continuous-process facilities. Capital per worker in the Japanese steel industry totaled $91,372 in 1978; the average in the United States was $40,486. The European figure is even less.[4] Similar ratios appear in the automobile and motorcycle industries.

Such production facilities contribute to productivity differentials and lead to cost advantages. In order to maximize cost advantages, Japanese firms also operate very large, centralized production plants. Toyota assembles three million cars per year in three plants. Ford's output of 3 million units is produced in more than twenty plants. In the steel industry, Nippon Steel operates a facility with an annual capacity of 17 million tons, an output greater than that of all but six nations. There are eight steel facilities in the world with capacity in excess of 10 million tons. All but one are Japanese facilities.[5]

Japanese firms also develop and use the most modern process technology in these facilities. In effect, these steps lead to the creation of an extremely steep cost curve. Japanese firms operate on the steepest possible curve, achieved through capital intensity and centralization of facilities. American firms, by contrast, often operate a number of smaller and less capital-intensive facilities. The result, as seen in Figure 1, can be a dramatic difference in direct factory costs. A comparable difference in other indirect costs also accompanies this approach to manufacturing.

Japanese firms carry significantly lower levels of inventory than do U.S. firms. This is not a result of the fact that Japanese suppliers hold the inventory for original equipment manufacturers (OEMs). That would merely

COMPARATIVE COST CURVES

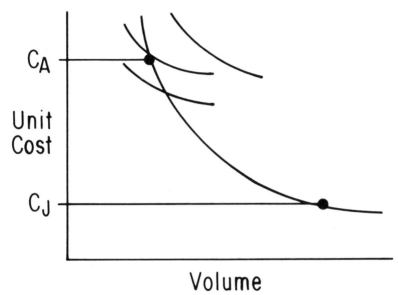

C_A

Unit
Cost

C_J

Volume

Figure 1 Comparative cost curves.

imply a shift in composition of inventory carrying. The fact is that Japanese industry as a whole carries much less inventory than does U.S. industry. This is accomplished in several ways. First, with fewer plants, the number of inventory holding points is reduced dramatically. Second, Japanese production schedules are far more inflexible than U.S. production schedules. As a result, the need for buffer stocks is greatly reduced. Third, Japanese companies tend to produce fewer models and to use standard components. The number of items in inventory is thus reduced significantly. Fourth, Japanese firms carry low finished goods inventory. Products move quickly from the factory to the end user. These factors reduce inventory requirements and lessen financing requirements. Perhaps more important, they cut factory overhead costs.

One recent private study found that Japanese compa-

Table 1   Materials Management and Quality Control
Comparisons in the United States and
Japanese Automobile Industries

	United States	Japan
Number of quality inspectors	1 per 7 workers	1 per 30 workers
Inventory/gross sales	GM—16.6%	Toyota—1.5%
Number of suppliers	GM—Over 3000	Toyota—300

SOURCE: From Yoshihiro Tsurumi, "Japan's Challenge to the United States," in W. H. Davidson and M. S. Hochmuth (eds.) *The New World Economic Order* forthcoming, 1984.

nies incurred unit purchasing, inventory, warehousing, transport, and logistics costs that were less than half those of similar American firms. Although Japanese firms have far higher "primary" overhead costs, those associated with fixed assets, their secondary overhead costs are much lower than those of U.S. companies. The study found that about 3 out of every 100 Japanese factory workers were engaged in the areas of purchasing, warehousing, distribution, and inventory management. The average number of workers involved in this function in the United States appears to be about 12 of every 100. This difference reduces indirect factory labor cost, but also dramatically reduces overhead. Although it varies by industry, up to one-third of total factory overhead can be attributed to these areas of activity.

Japanese firms can realize a major cost advantage because of their well-known inventory management (*kanban*) and supplier management practices.[9] One example of these results can be seen in a comparison of aggregate operating data in the automobile industry presented in Table 1. Note above that Toyota's inventory levels are 1.5% of sales compared to 16.6% for General Motors. Also, General Motors has more than 10 times as many suppliers as Toyota.

Another result of this centralized approach to manufacturing is consistent product quality. Centralized, automated facilities produce a product of extremely high consistency. Quality, defined here as a zero-defect product, is not simply a byproduct, however. Japanese firms have shown that increases in production yield reduce unit costs. Efforts to improve manufacturing yield are entirely consistent with the driving objective of cost reduction. Quality circle programs are an integral part of successful Japanese firms manufacturing strategies. Low prices and high quality, the Japanese trademarks, are a direct result of their manufacturing strategy.

Once the Japanese production system is in place, volume becomes critical to achieve cost leadership. All aspects of marketing activity are driven by the fundamental need to achieve volume and cost leadership. Penetration pricing, used to stimulate unit volume sales, is a common component of Japanese industrial strategies.

Marketing activities are conducted on a global basis, and mass distribution outlets are used to maximize volume. Other aspects of marketing activity also support cost leadership objectives. Product design tends to be standardized to maximize economies of scale in production. A relationship similar to that in Figure 1 also applies to the number of product models manufactured in any facility. Japanese firms tend to produce a smaller number of models

Table 2   Ball Bearing Sales and Product Line Statistics for Major Producers

	Total for Major Japanese Producers	Timken (United States)	SKF (Sweden)
Sales ($ million)	1,417	820	1,492
Number of models	10,000	12,500	25,000
Sales/model	141.7	65.6	59.7

SOURCE: I. C. Magaziner and T. M. Hout, *Japanese Industrial Policy,* London, Policy Studies Institute, 1980, p. 12.

in higher average unit volume than their Western counterparts. One example of this policy exists in the ball bearing industry. Japanese producers offer a significantly smaller number of "models," resulting in higher volume per product.

These brief overviews of manufacturing and marketing approaches help in understanding two key issues. First, they lead to additional criteria useful in selecting sectors for concentrated effort. Second, they begin to point out some of the problems and weaknesses of Japanese strategy.

SELECTION CRITERIA

We have already noted that low import cost to export value and high value-added ratios are key criteria for sector selection. The drive to achieve dominance through cost leadership creates several other key criteria. Cost leadership will be best achieved, given the strategy we have begun to outline, in industries with several characteristics. First, the product or its key components should be relatively standardized and homogeneous. Second, it should exhibit high unit volume. Third, demand should be highly price-elastic and price-sensitive. Cost structure is also important in sector selection. High value added is critical, but another issue is less apparent. What about margins? Are industries with high or low margins more attractive to the Japanese?

To address this issue, it is worthwhile to put the question of sector attractiveness within the framework of the familiar product cycle model (see Figure 2). The product life cycle is frequently segmented into four distinct phases: start-up, growth, maturity, and decline. Which of these stages will be most attractive to Japanese companies?

Consider the first stage of the cycle. The key success factors in this stage, those abilities that are critical to success, are product and market development. Neither have

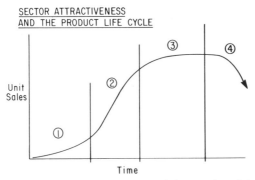

Figure 2   Sector attractiveness and the product life cycle.

been particular strengths of Japanese industry. In addition, stage 1 businesses do not exhibit high degrees of standardization, high unit volume, or price sensitivity. These qualities are most prevalent in stage 3 or 4 businesses.

Stage 3 businesses exhibit a very different set of key success factors. Costs become critical in such industries. Manufacturing efficiency is a critical success factor. Gross margins generally decline as businesses enter the third phase. This trend holds important implications. Low gross margins mean that manufacturing costs account for a significant share of total costs. If Japan wants to compete in sectors where manufacturing efficiency is critical, the single best criterion for selecting such sectors is low gross margins. When margins are low, manufacturing costs as a percentage of sales are high. If Japanese firms are more efficient at manufacturing, their cost advantage will be greatest in industries with low margins. Competitors also have less flexibility in industries with low margins. Penetration pricing will be most effective in industries with low margins, as competitors will be less able to absorb and meet price reductions.

These considerations make stage 3 businesses very attractive. They exhibit all the characteristics that support a strategy focused on dominance through cost leadership. However, there are several difficult problems with such sectors that must be addressed. Stage 3 businesses are subject to declining volume as markets obsolesce. In addition, the strategy employed by Japanese firms has other key weaknesses and vulnerabilities that can be developed by examining its historical roots.

The strategy defined above is not uniquely Japanese. It has been widely used by American firms. Its origins can be traced back directly to Dearborn, Michigan in 1906. Henry Ford's strategy in the automobile business was based on automated, capital-intensive manufacturing. Standardized units were produced in a continuous manufacturing process. The strategy was driven by the need to achieve high sales volume through mass marketing techniques. All production was centralized in the Rouge plant. Most important, Ford's pricing strategy was dictated by the need to achieve volume.

THE OLD MASTER

The roots of the strategy so successfully wielded by Japanese companies in the automobile, consumer electronics, and steel industries are distinctly American. Henry Ford was perhaps the master at its use. He first developed automated, high-volume production facilities that turned out a standardized product of consistent quality—the Model T. The car sold for $850 in 1906, when the average car sold for over $2000. Ford sold 6400 cars in 1907. By 1910, the price of the Model T had been reduced to $690 and volume was up to 34,500 units. In 1915, the car sold for $360, and 472,000 units were sold. Ford's market share rose from 15% in 1907 to 54% in 1913.[6]

Ford used the same strategy in entering the tractor industry in 1917. The Fordson tractor was introduced at a price of $750. International Harvester's cheapest model sold for over $900 at the time. Ford quickly captured 35% of the market by 1920. Then, in January 1921, David Lewis reports, "The company reduced the price of the Fordson to $625, a figure below the cost of producing it, in an effort to expand output, lower per-unit costs, and earn long-term profitability." In February 1922, Fordson prices were cut further to $395. General Motors, which had followed Ford in entering the tractor market, dropped out in October with a $33,000,000 loss. By the end of 1923, Ford unit sales had tripled the 1921 level and accounted for over 50% of the total market. Although Ford later lost its dominant positions in both the tractor and automobile industries to full-line producers, Ford revolutionized both industries by realizing the potential of mass production and marketing. Henry Ford has been quoted as saying that "price cuts were by far the most important [factor] in merchandising the Model T."[7]

AREAS OF VULNERABILITY

The strategy emerging here has been used before. It is good, old-fashioned American industrial strategy. The question is: How is it that Japanese competitors can use it so much more effectively than American firms? In order to answer this question, some of the problems associated with this generic strategy must be explored. Firms pursuing such a strategy are vulnerable in four critical areas: financing requirements, labor relations, competitive response, and product obsolescence.

Finances

Significant financing is needed to pursue this strategy. Huge initial investments in plant and equipment are required. Investments in working capital will be significant. Margins will be negative in the early stages of market penetration. Positive cash flows will not be achieved for many years. In this age of discounted cash flow analysis, the net present value of investments in such strategies can appear highly unattractive. This fundamental problem restricts the use of such a strategy by American companies. Japanese firms address this problem in several ways.

Financing requirements for working capital are extensive under this strategy. However, Japanese firms operate with markedly lower working capital requirements. Current assets in Japan, on average, exceed current liabilities by only 10%, while U.S. firms must finance significantly higher levels of current assets. The difference in working capital requirements stems in large part from inventory management practices.

The basic capital structure of Japanese industry is also very different from that of American industry. Aggregate financial data point out some of these differences. The most well-known and obvious difference is reflected in the debt–equity balance used to finance Japanese firms. On average, shareholders' equity accounts for 20% of the total capitalization of Japanese industry. Equity accounts for over 50% of the financial base of U.S. corporations.[8] Nonequity sources of finance are especially important to Japanese firms. Japanese capital markets are focused on the financing of fixed assets through long-term credits. The Industrial Bank of Japan, the largest bank in the country, finances such loans almost exclusively. The availability of low-cost, long-term debt supports investments in long-term industrial strategies.

As with other aggregate indicators, it is very important to look at individual industries and companies when examining financial statistics. Some of the differences between U.S. and Japanese computer companies can be seen in Table 3, but differences across and within industries in Japan are also apparent. The six leading Japanese computer manufacturers exhibit significantly higher debt–

equity ratios than do the consumer electronics companies. Inventory turnover is significantly lower in the Japanese computer industry than in the consumer electronics sector, and profitability is also lower.

The debt–equity ratio discrepancy provides the most important key for understanding how financial requirements are met in target sectors. Preferential access to low-cost debt is a critical means by which Japan concentrates its resources in target sectors. Firms in such sectors can

Table 3   Financial Ratios for Selected U.S. and
            Japanese Firms (1978)

Company	Debt–Equity Ratio	Profit/Sales	Inventory Turn Ratio
Burroughs	.538	10.46%	4.24
IBM	.538	14.76	6.24
NCR	.923	12.18	4.23
Control Data	.786	4.65	4.38
DEC	.639	9.90	3.58
Hitachi	2.99	2.56	5.45
Toshiba	5.08	1.52	3.56
Fujitsu	2.68	2.37	4.77
NEC	5.18	1.09	4.10
Oki	17.05	0.57	3.8
Mitsubishi Electric	5.67	1.71	3.78
Matsushita	1.01	3.34	16.47
Sanyo	2.02	1.93	21.32
Ricoh	1.43	4.15	12.10
Casio	1.60	3.54	7.82
Sony	.923	4.35	5.65
Sharp	2.125	2.76	9.64

SOURCE. *Sekai no Kigyo no Keiei Bunseki*, Industrial Policy Bureau, MITI, Tokyo, 1980, p. 29.

achieve debt–equity ratios of five to one or more. This type of extreme financial leverage can only be achieved in one way in the United States. The only U.S. firms exhibiting ratios comparable to those of leading Japanese firms are usually in or close to bankruptcy proceedings.

Japanese capital markets are willing to accept the risks associated with extreme financial leverage. The result is extreme financial leverage on top of extreme operating leverage in the production area. As a result, Japanese firms in target sectors have very high fixed costs. This cost structure drives industry to expand unit volume rapidly. After break-even volumes are achieved, massive positive cash flows can be realized. Until that position is reached, the financial requirements of the Japanese strategy are largely met by external debt financing, as reflected in high debt-to-equity ratios. The structure of U.S. capital markets limits U.S. firms' ability to execute this type of strategy. Labor markets are also an important constraint.

Labor Relations

Conditions in Japanese labor markets also provide a critical source of support for the generic strategy introduced by Henry Ford. Labor markets in the United States now limit American firms from following such an approach. In pursuing the strategy we have outlined, it is essential to maximize the centralization of production facilities. It is interesting to note that U.S. firms widely employ a "distributed," multifacility approach to production in serving world markets.[10] This strategy is highly distinct from the centralized Japanese approach. There are many good reasons for this distinction. Centralization of production facilities has four principal vulnerabilities. Centralized facilities are vulnerable to (1) changes in exchange rates, (2) import protection by host governments, (3) transportation problems or local cost increases, and—most important—(4) labor disruptions.

International Harvester restructured its manufacturing operations in 1976 to improve efficiency in the highly competitive agricultural equipment market. Facilities were rationalized so that individual components and products could be produced at a single location to maximize economies of scale. Manufacturing for engines, axles, and transmissions became highly centralized. Within two years of the transition, International Harvester was hit by a crippling strike which pushed the firm to the brink of bankruptcy.[11]

Japanese firms have a unique labor environment which permits centralization of facilities. The Japanese labor environment does more than permit such an approach. Labor in Japan is the most important source of both quality improvements and cost reductions.

Labor and capital markets in Japan provide powerful support for firms pursuing a strategy of centralization and automation. Access to low-cost capital has been a key factor in the success of export-oriented sectors in Japan. Its availability has stimulated the use of capital-intensive, automated, modern production facilities which contribute greatly to cost efficiency. This differential can be seen clearly in the automobile industry. One well-documented example involves a comparison of Ford and Toyo Kogyo (Mazda). As the figures in Table 4 indicate, Ford's production volume is greater than three times that of Toyo Kogyo. Experience curve analysis tells us that Ford's unit costs will be significantly below those of Toyo Kogyo. However, Ford's labor force is almost 10 times larger than its Japanese counterpart. This employment differential is larger than the gap in production. Ford requires over 100 hours of labor to assemble an automobile, compared to under 50 hours for Toyo Kogyo. Ford's hourly labor cost is also more than twice as high as its Japanese counterpart's. The end

Table 4   Comparison of Toyo Kogyo and Ford NAAO

	Ford NAAO	Toyo Kogyo
Production volume	3.163	0.983
Employees	219,599	24,318
Labor hours	355.75	46.20
Labor hours per vehicle	112.5	47.0
Hourly cost	$22.00	$10.45
Labor cost per vehicle	$2,464	$491
Adjustments		
For different size scale mix	1.38	1.00
Different degree of vertical integration	1.20	1.00
Labor cost per vehicle	$1,893	$589
Net differential		$1,304

SOURCE: W. J. Abernathy, K. B. Clark, and A. M. Kantrow, "The New Industrial Competition," *Harvard Business Review*, September–October 1981, pp. 80—81. See also, Yves Doz, *The World Automobile Industry*, in W. H. Davidson and M. S. Hochmuth (eds.) *The New World Economic Order*, forthcoming 1984.

result, after compensating for the larger unit size and higher degree of vertical integration at Ford, is a very significant cost differential. Toyo Kogyo's labor costs per vehicle are less than those of Ford Motor Company by something on the order of $1300.

This efficiency gap can be attributed to two broad categories of benefits. The first category includes economies derived largely from the physical plant and production process. The second category includes a set of human factors embodied in the labor force. These benefits would presumably accrue to the Japanese firm even if physical facilities and manufacturing processes were identical with those of an American facility. Two studies, one done by

Ford Motor (Study 2 in Table 5), the other by an academic team (Study 1 in Table 5), attempted to break down the cost differential into specific sources. The academic study attributes 34% of the $1300 differential to human factors; Ford's figure is 47%. In the extreme, however, it can be argued that almost all of these benefits can be attributed to labor relations conditions in Japan. Without a positive labor environment, it would be impossible for Japanese firms to rely on centralized facilities and constant process improvement to realize cost efficiency.

The Japanese are able to turn the inherent vulnerabili-

Table 5   Two Detailed Studies on the Cost Differential

	Sources of Cost Differential	
	Study 1	Study 2
Plant Engineering		
Process yield	40%	28%
Quality control	9%	5%
Technologies		
Automation	10%	6%
Product engineering	7%	6%
Human Resources		
Absenteeism	12%	18%
Broader job classifications and less supervision	18%	23%
Production rates	4% (?)	6%
Unallocated	—	8%
	100%	100%

SOURCE: Abernathy, (Clark and Kantrow (*op. cit.*); Doz (op. cit.).

ties of the generic Ford strategy into an advantage. They are able to handle the financial and labor relations vulnerabilities of their chosen strategy without difficulty. However, two other vulnerabilities pose additional problems. The most important of these perhaps is competitive response to their market activities.

Competitive Response

Sectors exhibiting the characteristics of high unit volume, low margins, standardization, and price sensitivity almost always correspond to mature, stage 3 or 4 businesses. Such businesses are typically dominated by well-established competitors. This poses a problem for a new entrant intent on achieving rapid volume growth. By definition, mature businesses exhibit little or no growth in aggregate unit volume. The only way to expand sales in such a market is to take share away from an established competitor. Any attempt to do so could be met by a vigorous response. If entrenched competitors resist penetration, and volume objectives are not met, there will be severe consequences for the new entrant. This is a critical problem for the Japanese. Determined resistance can postpone or prohibit achievement of cost leadership objectives. Japanese cost structures are extremely inefficient at low volume levels.

This weakness must be addressed if Japanese firms are to succeed in world markets. The key issue is determining the probability of vigorous competitive response. It will vary from sector to sector, depending on such factors as industry concentration and margins, and the postures and financial reserves of leading competitors. These factors can be considered in the sector selection process. More important, an entry strategy can be developed to minimize the probability of competitive response.

This can be accomplished by evaluating the posture of

established competitors. Firms in stage 3 markets share several characteristics. They will tend to be more concerned about increasing profits than about increasing unit sales. This tendency has an important effect on their activities in the market place. In order to realize improved profits, several main options exist. Earnings can be increased by cutting costs. This approach may require automation and modernization of facilities. Alternatively, sales and earnings can be increased by expanding market share. Each of these approaches poses problems.

Automation and modernization of facilities require investments that will lower reported return on investment. In this age of portfolio management, stage 3 or 4 businesses are often viewed as cash cows or worse. Management's objectives for such businesses will emphasize maximization of cash flow. Investment in such businesses is likely to be limited to maintenance requirements. The objective of increasing share is also problematic. Any attempts to increase share can lead to a competitive response that reduces margins and profits for everyone in the industry. Attempts to increase share through price reduction or increases in advertising, promotion, sales force, service, or improved terms will require margin reductions that squeeze profits in the short run. If competitors match these initiatives, market share and unit volume increases will not offset reductions in unit profit margins.

Another option for companies in mature businesses is diversification. Diversification offers an opportunity to use cash flows from a mature business to support development of a new growth business. This approach is the basis of good portfolio strategy, but it is extremely risky. Few firms duplicate past successes in new markets with regularity. Even under an active and successful diversification program, the objective of increasing profits and cash flows still applies to the original business. Also, for firms such as General Motors, Xerox, Zenith, and many others, the health of the original business will determine corporate performance almost regardless of the level of diversification efforts.

There is a much more attractive means of ensuring continued sales and profit growth. It involves no investment in facilities and can avoid the problems of competitive response. It can have an immediate positive effect on margins and profits. All it entails is raising prices. Of course, it is extremely difficult to raise prices on existing models. Price increases in such situations are generally introduced through model changes, optional features, improved performance, larger size, and premium packaging. In essence, the consumer is to be upgraded. If unit volume is flat, the only way to increase profits is to increase unit margins. That can best be accomplished by upgrading the user to a premium product. This path is almost irresistible to established competitors in stage 3 businesses. Most firms in an industry can readily perceive the logic of such an approach and will support efforts to move a market in this direction. The strategic momentum of established competitors in relatively concentrated industries almost always exhibits such a tendency.

Given this tendency, Japanese entrants can minimize the probability of competitive response. They can do so by focusing their efforts on a specific market segment. By extraordinary coincidence, that very segment happens to exhibit a perfect fit with other elements of Japanese industrial strategy.

There is a very powerful rationale for Japanese entry in the low price segment. This segment exhibits the greatest potential for standardization, highest unit volume, greatest price sensitivity, and lowest margins. Such products are most suited for sale in mass distribution outlets. Even more important, this segment generally will correspond closely in terms of product specifications to the Japanese home market, offering an opportunity to realize econo-

DYNAMIC MARKETING STRATEGIES

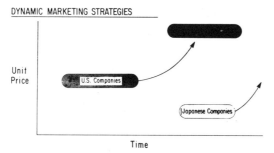

Time

Figure 3   Japanese entry strategy.

mies of scale. But these are only dividends. The key reason for entering in the low price segment is the fact that it ensures an ineffective competitive response. Established competition will almost always be unwilling or unable to compete successfully in this segment.

The U.S. auto industry's response to the invasion of low-priced German and Japanese imports provides an important example of this phenomenon. Many observers argue that the threat was initially ignored. It wasn't. The U.S. automobile companies, and particularly General Motors, largely upgraded their product lines between 1960 and 1970. The Chevrolet Impala increased in size during this period.[12] The range of models and options available increased sharply during this time.

This process is very similar to a phenomenon known as character displacement in population biology.[13] When two similar species compete for the same niche, it is common to find that the differences between the species become magnified in the area of overlap. General Motors avoided a direct confrontation by emphasizing the unique features of the traditional American automobile in size, sophisticated options, and model variety. Was it a good strategy?

In several respects, it was a very good strategy. First, General Motors had already established that this strategy could dominate an approach based on standardization and low prices when it surpassed Ford Motor in the 1930s.

Car consumers were willing to pay for size, options, and variety. GM had defeated Henry Ford before with such an approach; perhaps they could also defeat his emulators with the same strategy. Second, before the oil crisis, demand for small, fuel-efficient functional transportation was relatively limited. Most important, however, are the economics of the two major segments. General Motors, Ford, and Chrysler realized an average contribution margin per unit of more than $1200 in the early 1970s. Japanese firms realized average contributions on small cars at this time of about $400 per unit. If the U.S. car producers had succeeded in competing in the low price segment, they would have reduced their profitability dramatically, and they would have had to make major investments in order to do so.

Consider some hypothetical numbers. An established competitor has 40% of a six-million-unit market. Average margins are $1200. The firm's total contribution is $2.88 billion. Following the entry of new competitors in the low price segment, the firm vigorously markets a new line of small cars. As a result of these activities, the total market grows to eight million units. The dominant firm retains its 40% share, but half of its sales are now small cars. Its total contribution is now $1.92 billion from its traditional line ($1200 times 1.6 million units) plus the contribution from its small-car line. It is unlikely, however, that the firm will achieve unit contributions of $400 per small car because of higher unit costs. Even if this level is achieved, resulting in an additional $640 million in contributions ($400 times 1.6 million), total gross margin only reaches $2.56 billion, a reduction of $320 million. The results are highly unsatisfactory, and this is a relatively favorable scenario. The actual outcome depends on price–volume elasticity, cannibalization ratios, segment sizes, market shares, and the achievement of comparable efficiency in small-car production. No realistic combination of these variables results in a positive outcome for the established firm.

The bottom line of such simulated scenarios is quite clear. Established firms will be unwilling to compete aggressively in the low end of a market they have been attempting to upgrade. Even when they do compete in low price segments, it is likely to be a halfhearted response, as evidenced by the Corvair and Vega. This is true for a very simple reason. If established firms are successful in the low price segment, they will destroy their own profitability. This fundamental unwillingness to do battle in the low price segment provides an opportunity for market penetration. The potential problem of competitive response can be finessed by focusing on this segment.

Obsolescence

The Japanese appear to be able to deal with the principal vulnerabilities generally associated with their chosen approach. One additional problem must be addressed: the problem of obsolescence. Two related types of obsolescence, market and technological, are important. Market obsolescence can be thought of as the fourth stage of the product cycle. Declining volume need not be due to technological obsolescence. Many markets with long purchase cycles experience declines in unit volume as sales become dominated by replacement purchases. Nothing could be more frightening to a Japanese competitor than the prospect of declining market volume. This prospect is especially critical for firms which sell high-quality durable products. One of the problems with the Ford strategy is that it doesn't maximize repeat purchases. The GM strategy does, by planned model obsolescence and by promoting upgrading over the customer's life.

Technological obsolescence is also a problem. The strategy outlined above is vulnerable to changes in product technology. Product innovation could severely undermine marketing strategies, resulting in reduced volume and rising unit costs. Both prospects pose major risks and must be addressed if the strategy is to succeed. The Japanese solution to this problem underscores the dynamic nature of their strategy. It suggests a sequential approach to market dominance. In order to avoid obsolescence, Japanese firms gradually migrate from stage 3 segments to stage 1 segments in an industry. The television industry provides a classic example.

U.S. industry introduced black and white television in 1947. The first Japanese imports of black and white sets arrived in the United States in 1962, by which time the market had already peaked in terms of unit volume. Color televisions were first sold in significant numbers in the United States in 1960. The first Japanese imports arrived in 1967, some years before the peak in unit volume. The next important generations of television technology were solid-state circuitry and the video cassette recorder. Both were initially introduced by Japanese firms. Although Japanese firms entered the U.S. video market in a stage 4 segment, they gradually moved back into stage 2 and stage 1 segments. They now are the technological leaders in this industry. This example shows how Japanese industry deals with the threat of technological obsolescence.

This trend is also highly consistent with another evolving aspect of Japanese strategy. Although Japanese firms generally enter a market in the low price segment, they gradually move into the higher price segments. The benefits of upgrading are not lost on Japanese competitors. Where Ford and Volkswagen both almost went bankrupt because of inflexibility in the market place, Japanese firms are uniquely opportunistic. Over time, marketing activities evolve from a Ford mode to a General Motors mode, with rising emphasis on options, features, and model changes. Prices will rise accordingly and ultimately achieve premium levels as a reputation for quality spreads. If you've been to a Japanese car lot lately, this trend can readily be identified. Such an approach effectively deals with the threat of market obsolescence.

Japanese firms appear capable of addressing the principal weaknesses associated with a strategy focused on cost leadership. We must ask, however, if this is all there is to the famous "Japanese challenge." After all, this approach is relatively primitive in many respects. Can't other more refined and modern approaches be used to meet this challenge? The problem is that the Japanese approach is not simply a revamped version of Henry Ford's strategy. Several other factors must be considered in evaluating Japanese firms as competitors. The Japanese economic system provides uniquely powerful support to Japanese industry.

REFERENCES AND NOTES

1. The following table (on page 30) gives data on productivity-adjusted labor costs in the United States and Japan.
2. *A Note on the Motorcycle Industry,* Harvard Business School, 9–578–210, p. 16; "Strategy Alternatives for the British Motorcycle Industry," Boston Consulting Group, Boston, 1975.
3. See Table 2 and Table 4 in this chapter.
4. *Japanese Economic Yearbook,* 1977–1978, p. 133.
5. I.C. Magaziner and T.M. Hout, *Japanese Industrial Policy* (London: Policy Studies Institute, 1980), p. 13.
6. R.C. Epstein, *The Automobile Industry,* New York: Shaw and Company, 1928), app. A.
7. David L. Lewis, *The Public Image of Henry Ford* (Detroit: Wayne State University Press, 1976), pp. 180–181.
8. For a discussion see: Iwao Kuroda and Yoshiharu Oritani, "A Reexamination of the Unique Features of Japan's Corporate Financial Structure," *Japanese Economic Studies,* Summer 1980.
9. See for example: R. J. Schonberger, *Japanese Manufacturing Techniques* (New York: Free Press, 1982), *Productivity: The Japanese Formula* (New York: Arthur Anderson and Company, 1981).

A Comparison of Productivity-Adjusted Labor Costs in the United States and Japan (1970–1980)

Year	Average Annual Japanese Wages in Manufacturing[a] ÷	Japanese Output per Labor Hour Divided by U.S. Output per Labor Hour[b] =	Adjusted Japanese Labor Cost	U.S. Labor Cost[c]
1970	$ 1,787	0.508	$ 3,517	$ 7,439
1972	2,693	0.580	4,643	8,719
1974	4,224	0.649	6,508	9,947
1976	5,633	0.701	8,036	11,780
1978	10,009	0.782	12,799	14,063
1980	10,724	0.918	11,682	15,008

[a]These data cover the contracted cash payments to workers in manufacturing firms with 29 or more employees. From *Economic Statistics Annual*, Research and Statistics Department, Bank of Japan, 1981, pp. 293–294.
[b]This variable is created by dividing the average output per labor hour for Japanese industries by the average output in U.S. industries. Data are taken from the U.S. Department of Labor, Bureau of Labor Statistics.
[c]From Bureau of Labor Statistics, *Monthly Labor Review*, for manufacturing only.

10. W.H. Davidson, *Global Strategic Management* (New York: Ronald Press, John Wiley and Sons, 1982), Chapter 5.
11. "The Strike that Rained on Archie McCardell's Parade," *Fortune*, August 13, 1978.
12. *Consumer Reports*, Annual Automobile Survey, 1960 and 1970.
13. E.O. Wilson, *Sociobiology* (Cambridge: Harvard University Press, 1978).

2

The Japanese
Economic System

One of the most widely observed attributes of Japanese strategy is its long-term orientation. Japanese firms are willing to forego short-term profits in order to maximize profits in the long run. This observation is often supported by a comparison of U.S. and Japanese entry pricing strategies. American firms follow a skimming strategy to maximize short-term profit, while Japanese firms invest in market share, while reducing costs, to maximize long-term profits. This observation is relevant to any analysis of Japanese strategy, but it is important to go a step beyond. It is only a half truth that Japanese firms are willing to forego short-term profits to make long-term profits. The whole truth is that Japanese firms are willing to forego profits, period. Japanese firms are willing to accept lower profits over any time frame. Their return-on-investment criteria are far lower than those of U.S. firms.

Figure 4 charts the relative profitability of U.S., European, and Japanese firms from 1970 to 1979. These data, from MITI studies, show that the average return on total assets for Japanese firms is far below that of U.S. industry. These figures are for Japanese industry as a whole, and significant deviations from sector to sector should be expected. The key point is that, over time, Japanese

31

Figure 4   Corporate profits in four countries—average return on profits for manufacturing firms in the United States, the United Kingdom, West Germany, and Japan. From *Sekai no Kigyo no Keiei Bunseki*, Industrial Policy Bureau, MITI, Tokyo, 1980, p. 20.

industrial profitability is actually declining. The gap between average returns for Japanese and American firms has increased in the past decade.

This is a critical observation. Why should Japanese industry be willing to accept a lower return on assets than U.S. firms? Several factors can explain this differential. First, Japanese firms have a lower cost of capital. Restrictions on the outflow of capital, and on the use of Japanese credit facilities by foreign borrowers, maintain an artificially low cost of capital in Japan.[1] Lower capital costs permit Japanese firms to accept lower returns on investment. Second, leverage rates in Japan on average are twice those found in the United States, resulting in returns on equity that are actually about two-thirds of those in the United States. Third, the primary source of funds in Japan, the banking system, is primarily concerned with long-term debt coverage, not profits. Shareholders, the dominant sources of finance in the United States, are primarily concerned with short-term returns. Nonetheless, return on total capital is a critical indicator of industrial performance. An additional factor must be considered to explain why Japan is willing to accept a lower return on capital. It is important to consider how corporate profits are used in Japan and the United States. A very large share of corporate profits in the United States goes to the Federal Government in the form of taxes. These revenues are used to fund a federal budget that consists primarily of defense and social welfare expenditures. In Japan, federal expenditures are far lower than in the United States, totaling 11.5% of GNP, compared to about 23% in the United States in 1981.[2] This differential is largely due to lower defense and social welfare expenditures in Japan. The private sector carries a larger proportion of social welfare responsibilities in Japan than it does in the United States. Individuals, families, and corporations have carried a large part of the burden.[3]

Once the private sector assumes partial responsibility for welfare programs, corporate profitability requirements change dramatically. U.S. corporate profits in the manufacturing sector in 1980 totaled $74.5 billion, while federal transfer payments in 1980 totaled $283.7 billion.[4] The existence of a separate, government-run welfare system requires high profits and taxes for support. Once the welfare delivery apparatus or a large part of it is folded into industry, the nation no longer needs high profits to fund a parallel welfare system. From another perspective, once these "social costs" are added to corporate expenses, reported profits will decline. Japanese corporate profits were $41.4 billion in 1980; their federal transfer payments totaled $52.2 billion.[5]

Welfare levels are clearly lower in Japan than in the United States; the Japanese economic system as a whole carries a significantly lower welfare burden than the U.S. system.[6] However, in delivering any given level of welfare benefits, the corporate system may be able to handle welfare programs far more efficiently than a parallel public system can. This approach also ensures productive contributions to the national economy because individuals associate their own long-term security with the success of their employers. The bottom line is this: So long as social welfare functions are performed by industry, reported profits will be far lower than they will be in countries with separate public welfare systems. Profit requirements will also be lower. From the national perspective, low profits and a low public welfare burden can be superior to high profits and a high public welfare burden.

The corporate system does not provide welfare services to all Japanese citizens. The celebrated lifetime employment system does not apply to the average Japanese worker. This system is widely used in the top tier of Japanese industry. Employees of Hitachi, Mitsui, NEC, Nippon Steel and so on do enjoy these benefits. However, the bulk of the Japanese work force is employed by smaller, second-tier companies, many of whom are suppliers to the top firms. Over 75% of all Japanese workers are employed by firms with less than 1000 workers.[7] Job security in these firms is very limited. Japan has traditionally had the highest rate of corporate bankruptcy in the world. For most Japanese, low job security means two things. First, they must work hard to ensure the long-term success of their employers. Second, ultimately, they must provide their own welfare safety net. They respond by saving a very high percentage of their income. The well-known savings differential between the United States and Japan can be attributed largely to the structure of the Japanese welfare system.

These savings provide a large pool of low-cost capital available for financing Japanese industry. Restrictions on

Table 6   Corporate Bankruptcies
in the United States and
Japan

| | Number of Cases | |
Year	United States[a]	Japan[b]
1973	9,345	9,349
1974	9,915	11,738
1975	11,432	13,224
1976	9,628	16,606
1977	7,919	17,987
1978	6,619	15,575
1979	7,564	16,517
1980	11,742	18,212
1981	25,346	17,397

[a]Council of Economic Advisors' *Economic Report to the President*, February 1982, p. 338.
[b]*Economic Survey of Japan*, 1980–1981, p. 106. *New York Times*, April 13, 1982, p. 106. sect. 4, p. 26.

outflows of savings and on borrowing by foreigners in Japan ensure that the cost of these funds remains below world standards. The capital markets in Japan provide these funds at advantageous rates to target sectors, identified in the industrial planning exercises involving MITI, Keidanren, the Ministry of Finance, and other actors.

The structure of the Japanese system forces a subsidy from savers to borrowers. The system restricts the flow of funds abroad, and limits internal access by foreign borrowers.[8] This pattern is entirely consistent with other aspects of the Japanese economic system that support industry and labor at the expense of consumers and other segments of society. Another clear example of this approach can be seen in the allocation of capital to housing in Japan. The biggest single user of capital in the United States since 1945 has been the residential housing sector. The average U.S. home buyer could generally borrow long-term, fixed-rate money at rates similar to those available to General Motors during this period. In Japan, home buyers have limited access to "public" funds, and they pay a far higher relative price for those funds than their U.S. counterparts.[9] Japanese capital markets are designed to provide a powerful source of support for Japanese industry. The important immediate result is a willingness to accept a far lower return on investment than their U.S. competitors are willing to accept. This fundamental ability, perhaps more than any other factor, can explain the origins and success of Japanese industrial strategy. Labor markets are also structured to provide a powerful source of support to industry.

JAPANESE LABOR RELATIONS

Although labor relations in Japan seem placid, passive, and positive by American standards, there is a long history of turbulence in this area. The trade union movement grew rapidly during the American occupation, and was a powerful force in the immediate postwar years. Union membership grew from 365,000 in 1939 to 6,677,000 in 1948. With rising membership came rising militancy. A general strike was called in 1947. A centralized union organization, Sohyo, was formed in 1950. This organization implemented five nationwide 24-hour walkouts in 1952, in support of wage demands involving up to three million workers. Additional national walkouts were held in 1953.[10]

Despite the apparent early strength of the labor movement, a number of forces have acted to reduce organized labor's role in Japanese industry and politics. First, the government established that it would take forceful action when necessary to curtail labor unrest. The 1947 general strike was effectively canceled when General MacArthur revoked the right to strike for public employees. The government also took strong measures to limit the impact of the labor unrest of 1952 and 1953. The so-called "red purges" of this period are one example. The 1948 Labor Relations Adjustment Act and the 1949 Dodge Plan strengthened the power of management to limit labor disruptions. Union membership began to decline in 1949 and continued to do so through the mid-1950s. Second, an organization of employers called Nikkeiren was formed in 1948. This organization is somewhat similar to the Keidanren organization. However, where Keidanren focuses on relations with government, the political interests of industries, and industry's input to the national planning process, Nikkeiren focuses on labor relations issues. This organization provides a united management front in dealing with labor relations issues.

By contrast, the union movement is highly fragmented. The central organization, Sohyo, lost splinter groups consistently in the 1950s. Major defections occurred in 1953, including the textile workers, who represented over 20% of total employees at the time. This fragmentation occurred at precisely the same time that the AFL–CIO merger in 1955 established central union leadership in the United States. By the late 1950s fewer than half the more than 66,000 unions in Japan belonged to any central union organization.[11]

The fragmentation of the union movement is a key factor in evaluation of Japanese industrial relations. There are several reasons for the high level of fragmentation. Over three-fourths of all Japanese union members belong to unions that operate solely within one company.[12] The focus of these unions on company issues limits industry-wide collective bargaining, which is a rarity in Japan. In addition, the prevalence of joint management–labor councils at the company level defuses union power to represent workers. Many worker welfare functions are handled by joint worker–management councils, groups such as the Dormitory Club, or other company-sponsored groups.

The paternalism of Japanese industry also works against union power. Many companies continue to pay workers when they are on strike. Bonuses are common when workers return to their jobs. Such an approach was critical in the resolution of a major strike at Nissan in 1954. In general, management attitudes toward workers are more supportive and conciliatory than they are in the United States. In an extreme case, a major strike at Toyota in the late 1950s was resolved when the entire board of directors resigned, admitting failure to manage labor relations properly.

Another factor underlying the positive labor relations environment is the widespread attitude that strikes are not a test of strength, but a means of communication to management. This belief is underlined by a widespread cultural aversion to formal contracts and arbitration. It is well known that few disputes in Japan are settled in court by lawyers. Japanese custom focuses on resolving disputes directly. This principle applies in the labor relations area. External arbitration of labor disputes is extremely rare in Japan. Management and labor work together to settle these issues in direct communication.

An additional factor to be considered is the traditional low labor mobility in Japan. Finally, since the 1949 Dodge Plan, the focus of wage determination has been on productivity improvements. Wage increases are tied to increases in worker productivity. Management and labor have a common interest in improving productivity. At the national level, this joint interest was symbolized in 1955 when Keidanren invited major unions to join in the creation of the Japanese Productivity Center. At the enterprise level, management and labor work closely together to enhance productivity. Joint councils are a key mechanism for pursuing this objective. These mechanisms are critical in understanding the success of the Japanese industrial system. I had the opportunity to view such a system at work in a leading Japanese company. The following example offers insight into the structure and functions of these management systems.

SMALL-GROUP ACTIVITY AT MUSASHI SEMICONDUCTOR WORKS

Musashi Semiconductor Works is Hitachi Corporation's oldest and largest semiconductor factory. Located less than one mile from Hitachi's central research laboratory in the suburbs of Tokyo, the present facility grew out of a small transistor research center and pilot plant created in 1958. Today Musashi employs 2700 workers and manufactures semiconductor memory and logic devices, microcomputers, and computer boards.

Musashi, like the rest of Hitachi's 27 Japanese factories, employs a formal small-group activity program. This program must be differentiated from the prevailing U.S. concept of the quality circle. Hitachi's concept of small-group activity encompasses a much broader range of activities than those normally associated with quality circles. Quality circles, or small groups whose primary purpose is to improve and control product quality, account for about 29% of all small-groups within Hitachi. Another 4% of all small groups are principally concerned with worker safety. The remainder focus on what are called management improvement (MI) activities.[13] The focus of MI groups can be broadly described as operations management and refinement. It is important to note that small-group activity in Japan encompasses not only production workers but also clerical, support, and certain managerial personnel. Regardless of the area of activity, MI groups play an important role in designing and refining operating, administrative, and organizational systems.

Although the origin of small-group systems can be traced

directly to American statistical quality control and Scanlon Plan techniques, other factors influencing the development of these systems are distinctly Japanese.[14] Perhaps the most important indigenous base for such systems can be found in the tradition of the *habatsu*. The Japanese word *batsu* means "group." The *habatsu* is an ancient Japanese unit of military organization. A *habatsu* unit typically consisted of six men who lived and fought together as a "fighting clique." These units have been the basis of military organization and strategy in Japan for centuries. This tradition, in combination with other well-known Japanese cultural qualities, provided a firm foundation for the adoption of small-group systems. Examination of small-group activities at Musashi Semiconductor Works provides insight into the distinctly Japanese nature of these systems.

Implementation of a Small-Group Program

The implementation of a small-group program at Musashi began in 1971. Hitachi Corporation had already initiated programs at 14 other factories, and procedures for designing and implementing small-group systems at the plant level were well established. There are two distinct phases of implementation. The first phase focuses on management orientation and development of the philosophy and values underlying small-group programs. The second phase focuses on introducing the program at the worker level.

The initial stage of implementation at Musashi, which occurred between 1971 and 1975, is called the enlightenment period. This period focuses almost entirely on the orientation of management. Managers are trained and oriented in the philosophy, principles, structure, and function of small-group activities. Formal education programs play a key role in management orientation. Distinct programs are held for each level of management. These programs are often conducted at remote sites. In most cases, the instructors are corporate personnel. In some companies, members of the corporate board of directors play key roles as instructors. Although individual courses can last up to six months, most of them last less than one month. In the case of Musashi, it took over three years to complete the entire management orientation program.

The small-group concept was introduced by management to the rest of the organization in 1975. At the worker level, the small-group program was implemented as part of a broader campaign designed to improve dramatically the status and productivity of Musashi Works. This broader campaign, called the MMM movement, entailed no specific organizational or managerial innovations. It was intended to provide continuing themes, rallying points, and broad goals throughout the process of initiating the small-group program. The MMM movement refers to three words: *muda, mura, muri*. These words were used to symbolize a new guiding theme for Musashi Works. They can be translated respectively as waste, inconsistency, and excess. The purpose of the MMM movement is to eliminate these three evils from Musashi Works.

Several phases of the MMM movement at Musashi can be identified. In the first phase, between 1975 and 1976, the focus of the MMM movement was on achieving higher quality in manufacturing through reduction of the three evils. In the second phase, between 1976 and 1977, MMMII's theme was that by reducing the three evils, Musashi could spring forward to become a factor in world industry. The objective of the third phase, between 1977 and 1978, was more specific: The MMM20 campaign was designed to increase efficiency in terms of output per worker by 20% in six months. After this specific objective had been met, another general objective was introduced: The MMM80 campaign, between 1978 and 1980, sought to challenge and defeat the top-line brands of the world through reduction of the three evils. In 1981, a new theme with a specific objective was introduced: The MMM200 UP program intends to double chip output in two years.

The MMM movement appears to have been an important instrument in introducing small-group activity at the worker level. However, this campaign is only the very tip of the iceberg. Underlying it is a complex and sophisticated organization built around the small-group unit.

Small Group Organization and Administration

The 2700 workers at Musashi are organized into 360 groups. A typical group numbers 8 to 10 people. Group membership is determined largely by work stations, although some self-selection is possible in certain work areas. Group members typically hold the same rank or position in the company, but groups are often of mixed sex and age. Small-group systems are highly democratic at the group level, with each group electing a leader from among its members.

Immediately above the small-group level, a formal hierarchy is developed to administer group activities. This hierarchy is composed of councils, and it closely parallels the overall formal structure of the Musashi organization. Each of the 20 departments within Musashi has its own department council, which is chaired by the department manager and which includes senior departmental managers as members. Further, each department contains between 2 and 10 sections. Separate councils are formed for each of these sections, with participants drawn from the full range of the departmental hierarchy. This range includes senior departmental managers as well as foremen and workers. Section councils thus serve as the most important forum for information exchange; they facilitate communication between all levels of the organization. Figure 5 shows the structure of the small-group system.

Hitachi views these section councils as a means of communicating policies and objectives from management

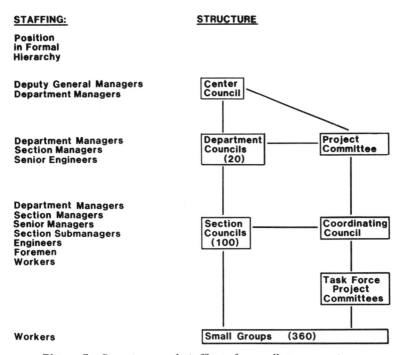

Figure 5   Structure and staffing of a small-group system.

to the rest of the organization, particularly to the group level. Section councils set specific objectives and themes for individual groups and review each group's performance on a monthly basis. However, it is very important to emphasize that communication between a council and a worker group is a two-way exchange.

Worker groups are assigned objectives and themes by their section council, but they also choose a separate theme for themselves. These groups have a great deal of latitude, self-direction, and autonomy in Hitachi's program. The sole constraint on group activities is that they be broadly consistent with the objectives of the divisional management and Hitachi Corporation. Within the framework of the MMM movement at Musashi, worker groups are given equal responsibility with management for submitting management improvement suggestions. The conceptual framework for the overall small-group activities movement is presented in Figure 6.

The task force projects cited in Figures 5 and 6 are an important element in small-group programs. Although the primary focus of small-group programs is on generating self-selected proposals from worker groups, management also has mechanisms to direct group efforts toward specific projects. Following the establishment of channels for submission of group proposals, department and section

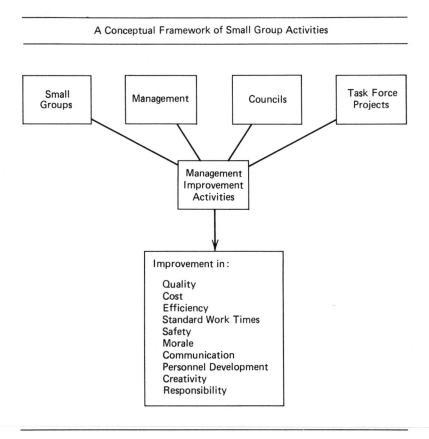

Figure 6   A conceptual framework of small-group activities.

councils identify special areas and projects for specific attention. A committee structure is used to manage these special project activities. Depending on the priorities established in the center council, an individual group could find itself working primarily with a project task force committee, rather than on self-selected improvements. These specific projects are defined and initiated by management, and implemented through the project committee shown in Figure 5. Since many task force projects involve multiple worker groups, sections, and departments, a coordinating council is used to promote cooperative efforts in such projects.

In addition to communicating policies and objectives from management to workers, Hitachi describes the section councils as a means of achieving "technology transfer" from small groups to the management level. The vehicle for transferring technology, and indeed the focal point of the entire small-group program, is called the improvement proposal.

Improvement Proposals

Improvement proposal generation, evaluation, and implementation within a small-group activity program are part of an extremely sophisticated process with far-reaching implications. An improvement proposal is first submitted formally by a group to a section council. The proposal includes a statement of the problem, a proposed solution, and, in many cases, a description of actual results achieved under the new method. Proposals need not be approved before they are executed unless they involve major capital expenditures or adjustments at other work stations. If adjustments are required at other stations, section and departmental approval are required, and implementation is overseen by the coordinating council.

The first improvement proposals were filed within Musashi Works in 1977, six years after the program began.

Translation of an Improvement Proposal

Sec-tion	Item	Improvement of Heat Sealing Process for LSI Semiconductors				
No.	Date	The 10th month of the 55th year of Emperor Hirohito's reign (1980)	Cost savings	¥140,000 per month	Capital invested	¥3 (Mill.)

Before Improvement

In the sealing process for final LSI preparation, the following problems occur:

1. The efficiency of the sealing oven is low because of the need to space units entering it (see flow chart).
2. Two people are required for inserting and removing units from the oven. Each has to wait in between units because of spacing requirements.

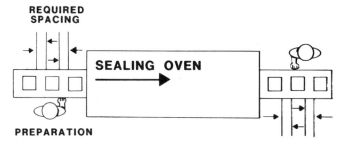

REQUIRED SPACING

SEALING OVEN

PREPARATION

Steps in old process:

1. Preparation: manually place units in staging area.
2. Manually place units on oven conveyor belt.
3. Wait for proper spacing of next unit.
4. Place next unit on conveyor belt.
5. Sealing takes place within the oven.
6. Manually remove unit from oven.
7. Place unit in box for transport to final packing area.
8. Wait
9. Remove next unit

Figure 7 Translation of an improvement proposal.

Name of Group Leader	K. Sukiya	Unit	Department AB: Prototype Development	Group Name	H&S	Tel.	683
Area involved in application	Prototype design		Engineering application	MD activities			

After Improvement

By analyzing the thermal requirements and characteristics of the sealing process, it was possible to develop a temperature and time cycle that eliminates the need for spacing. This results in an increased speed of production, and it permits automation of the insertion and removal of units from the oven (see flow chart).

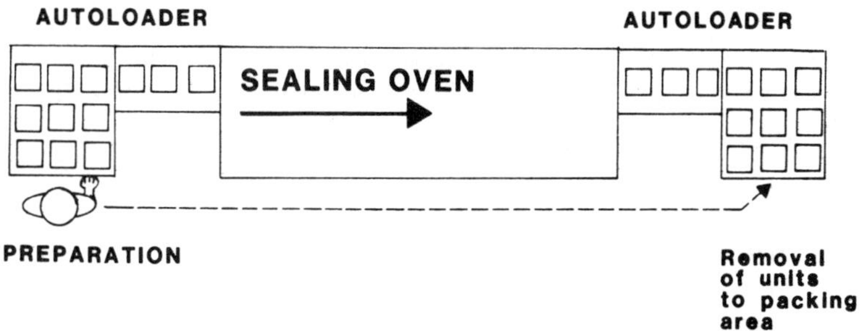

AUTOLOADER   AUTOLOADER

SEALING OVEN

PREPARATION

Removal of units to packing area

Steps in new process:
1. Preparation: manually place units in staging area.
2. Insertion into oven done by autoloader.
3. Sealing takes place.
4. Removal done by autoloader.
5. Place units in box for transport to packing area.

Figure 7 (Continued)

Initially, small groups were encouraged to identify areas within their work stations that could be improved to further the MMM movement. Thus, the first improvement proposals were voluntary. Over time, the scope of self-selected improvement activities was broadened significantly. By 1980, section councils were asking groups to commit themselves to filing a certain number of improvement proposals each month. The targeted number of proposals was negotiated individually with each group, but competition and peer pressure clearly played a role in this process.

Improvement proposals are typically filed on hand-written sheets of paper. A translated example of a proposal appears in Figure 7. In this case, the proposal suggests a change in the design of work stations and work flow in the large scale integrated (LSI) chip sealing process. The proposal involves reduction of the number of work steps and the elimination of one employee per station.

Each group submits a monthly review of its activities in addition to individual proposals. These monthly reviews serve as the principal vehicle for control and feedback from management. Reviews are presented on poster-sized paper and often contain interesting and creative artwork. These documents provide perhaps the best insight into the inner workings of the small-group system.

The Bandits

Figure 8 offers insight into the dynamics of the small-group system. This figure presents a group of three men and three women who work in the photolithography section of the integrated circuit (IC) production department. Their job is to transfer circuitry from master photomasks to photosensitized silicon wafers. The box in the upper right-hand corner gives the department and section, the group leader's name, and the chosen name of the group: the Bandits.

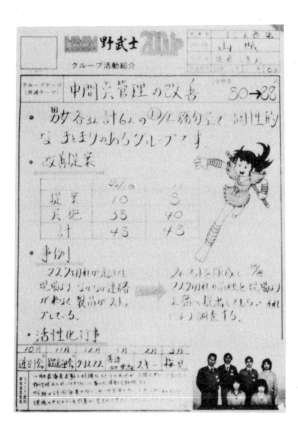

Figure 8   The bandits.

The long rectangular box at the top gives the group's theme and goal: improvement of photolithography management and an increase in chip yield at this stage from 80% to 88%. Below the rectangle, the group introduces itself. They say they are individuals with strong personalities, but the members work well together. The numbers in the box show the group's level of improvement proposal activity in the tenth and eleventh months of the fifty-fifth year of Emperor Hirohito's reign. In October, the group submitted 10 suggestions for discussion and implemented 38 improvements. In November, the group submitted 8 proposals and implemented 40 improvements. Below the box, an example of one of their proposals is cited. The example states that mask deterioration is often not noticed until after chip output is affected. Implanted impurities accumulate as photomasks are used, resulting in defects on individual integrated circuits and reduced yields. The group developed a new format in conjunction with the photomask department to test masks weekly for impurities to reduce this problem.

The bottom area of this poster includes the group's plans for joint activities along with supervisor comments. The group held a farewell party in October, a welcome party in November, and a Christmas party in December; they are planning a show or movie in January, a skiing trip in February, and a Plum Blossom picnic in March. At the very bottom are the supervisor's comments: "Your group was announced to be the best group in October. I am expecting this group to continue its energetic activities. For the last half of this year, your group will stay on the Special Project Team [i.e., report to a Project Task Force Committee]. I know it is very hard to work on Special Projects, but very important improvements will result. Good luck."

The Ten Philosophers

One further example of a monthly review is useful in understanding how the small-group system works. Figure 9 presents another group called the Ten Philosophers. The group's statement is presented in the same general format as the Bandits' in Figure 8. The group comes from the wafer processing section of the IC memories manufacturing department. Their theme and objective is reduction of foreign matter (e.g., dust) in ICs. Below the theme box is a circle. The words inside the circle ask: "What is a philosopher?" The answer is given in four parts. First, he is a

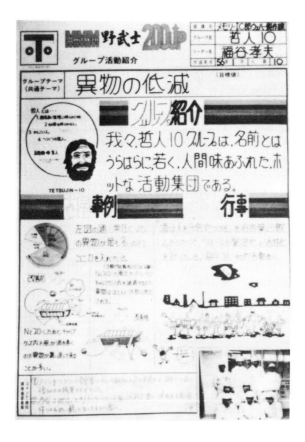

Figure 9   The Ten Philosophers.

person who knows the world and what he should and shouldn't do. Second, he is a person who deserves respect. Third, he is wise. Finally, he is a master of distorted logic. The caption concludes: "Therefore, we must be weirdos, no?"

Parallel to the photograph is an introduction to the group that states: "We are ten philosophers, like our name says. We are young, human, and enthusiastic personnel." Under the striped lines on the left is an example of an actual improvement that was implemented by the group. The pie chart shows that the areas of highest probability of wafer contamination are in the deposition of thin insulating and conducting films through chemical vapor deposition (CVD) or evaporation processes. Impurities introduced in these processes can become implanted in the silicon, destroying the integrity of circuits and causing reduction in chip yield. To reduce contamination, the group has implemented a new system in which gases pass through filter screens.

To the right of the improvement example, along with some artwork created by the group, is the statement, "Our key phrase is 'drinking makes everyone friends.' Therefore we drink and sing a lot to improve our group. In addition, we have other activities once a month." Below this statement are the supervisor's comments. He states: "By focusing on communication, you are trying to improve group unity. In most respects, your performance is double that of other groups. In the future, try to improve your contact with other groups. You should be an example for other groups and teach them."

Mechanisms for Achieving Management Objectives

The improvement proposal submitted by individual groups is the key mechanism for achieving management objectives as outlined in the MMM movement. Based on themes suggested by management, small groups propose improvements that are then translated into specific projects. Thus, management support of the small-group program, coupled with what Hitachi calls total employee participation, creativity, and aggressive spirit, leads to specific benefits in morale, quality, and efficiency, including improvements in inventory levels and standard production times.

Improvement proposals are the core of the small-group programs, but these programs contain two other pathways for achieving management objectives. The first is called direct employee action. In the case of Musashi, introduction of the broad MMM theme stimulated better morale and directly resulted in cleaner facilities and higher efficiency. This result might be correlated with the widely discussed Hawthorne Effect known to U.S. managers. Second, the project committee mechanism for implementing management-initiated improvements also plays a critical role in achieving specific management objectives.

Results of the Small-Group Activity Program

The first formal improvement proposals were filed at Musashi Works in 1977. In 1978, 26,543 specific proposals were filed. Since that time, the number of proposals has increased dramatically. In the first half of 1979, 47,347 proposals were submitted. In the second half of 1980, 112,022 proposals were submitted by the 360 worker groups within the Musashi factory. Of this total, 98,347 improvements were implemented by the end of the year. The average group completed about 45 improvements per month between July and the end of December 1980.

The completed improvements can be broken down into several categories. Of the 98,347 improvements completed, 26% resulted in a reduction of standard times at individual work stations. An additional 27% resulted in the reduction of inventory. Safety improvements and overhead cost savings each accounted for 6% of the completed improvements. Efficiency improvements in office and clerical functions were the focus of 24% of the completed proposals, which reflected small-group activity away from the factory floor. The remaining proposals were largely devoted to increasing yields at various stages of production.

Although the level and intensity of small-group activity appear remarkable by Western standards, Musashi only achieved the average level of activity for Hitachi as a whole in 1980. Activity in this case is measured in terms of the annual number of proposals completed per worker.

Although Hitachi is a leading user of small-group systems, activity levels at Hitachi should not be viewed as unrepresentative of Japanese industry. In 1979, a number of Japanese companies exhibited higher levels of small-group activity. Below are listed four of these companies and the number of proposals submitted by each worker:

Aishin Seiki—56 proposals per worker
Aishi Warner—44 proposals per worker
Fuji Electric—99 proposals per worker
Pentel—43 proposals per worker

As a whole, Hitachi Corporation received an average of 39 proposals per worker.

THE BOTTOM LINE

As the example of Musashi Works demonstrates, Japanese small-group activity systems are painstakingly and patiently nurtured into a highly sophisticated and powerful structure for achieving specific and general management objectives. Worker participation is encouraged through peer pressure, group affiliation benefits, and the intergroup competition inherent in the system. The group structure is used to formalize specific objectives and commitments consistent with overall management strategy at all levels of the organization.

The record of small-group activities at Musashi Works indicates the tremendous potential of such programs in improving operating results. These activities systematize and accelerate the realization of learning curve benefits in all aspects of operations. As a force for improved efficiency and quality, small-group activity represents one of the most important competitive advantages of the Japanese industrial system. Such activities are particularly important in industries such as the semiconductor industry, where technical change is frequent and process evolution is rapid.

The applicability of small-group systems in foreign settings remains to be seen.[15] Many of the strengths of such systems are rooted in Japanese culture and society. Although underlying worker attitudes and norms are important, Japanese firms use very sophisticated systems and structures for promoting employee motivation, dedication, and productivity. These systems, built upon an advantageously organized labor market, provide a critical source of support for Japanese industrial activities.

NATIONAL PLANNING AND RESOURCE ALLOCATION STRUCTURES

One final observation on the Japanese system requires development. The Japanese "indicative" planning system involves close and intense interaction among business and government groups in creating and implementing industrial policy. The Ministry of Finance, MITI, and Keidanren are the principal but by no means the only representatives of business and government interests in setting priorities for industrial sectors. Joint determinations by these institutions do not exclude divergent activities by other business and government parties. However, the formal priorities emerging from MITI and Keidanren deliberations are the basis for identifying target sectors. Several key bureaus within MITI and the Finance Ministry are major actors in these processes. The Industrial Policy Bureau within MITI is central in establishing the broad direction of Japanese industrial policy. This broad direction was presented in a 1980 MITI publication entitled *A Vision for the 1980s*, which identifies "knowledge-intensive industries in general and specific sectors such as information processing and aerospace" as areas for future expansion. At a more basic level, MITI's Price Policy Division recommends which industries, firms, and projects receive low-cost funds. Within the Ministry of Finance, the Fiscal Investment and Loan Plan Bureau (FILP), one of seven major bureaus, channels federal funds into target sectors, firms, and projects. In the capital markets themselves, the Finance Ministry's Banking Bureau controls the Bank of Japan. The central bank has a close relationship with the 13 larger city banks that account for over 50% of all commercial bank assets in Japan.[16] The Bank of Japan and another public bank, the Japan Development Bank, play key roles in directing bank loans to sectors.

Target sectors are not identified solely by MITI analysts. These priorities emerge after lengthy and intense debate, structured to ensure complete and competitive analysis of alternatives. Part of this process occurs within MITI itself. MITI is organized into trade bureaus responsible for evaluation of individual industries. These trade bureaus analyze international opportunities and assess the attractiveness of individual sectors. The interaction of bureau "champions" within MITI is one of the most important determinants of sector prioritization in Japan. A similar process occurs in the private sector. The Keidanren, or Federation of Economic Organizations, represents the industrial establishment in industrial policy debates. This institution consists of about 750 corporate members, and is internally organized by industry sectors. Each sector presents its own case for priority status in competition with other sectors. There is also a high degree of interaction with the counterpart bureau within MITI in making a case for emphasizing any given sector.[17]

The priorities emerging from the MITI–Keidanren deliberations, with additional inputs from other government agencies, business interests, and academics, form the basis for resource allocation in Japan. High-priority sectors can receive preferential treatment in terms of direct grants, tax benefits, public purchases, protection against imports, and access to low-cost capital. With so much at stake, political considerations might be expected to dominate the process of selecting target sectors. One important structural consideration limits this sort of activity. Japanese industry is dominated by the remnants of the prewar Zaibatsu groups. These large industrial groups are the key members of Keidanren. Each group is active in virtually the entire range of industries in Japan. Since each firm will be represented in high-priority sectors, defensive political actions in support of low-priority sectors will be limited. The structure of Japanese industry thus limits compromise and stimulates concentration in resource allocation.

The immediate result is a two-tier economy. Target sectors receive tremendous benefits while low-priority industries receive very limited national support. As a result, some Japanese industries are extremely competitive by international standards while others operate at a severe disadvantage. The magnitude of the differential between low- and high-priority sectors can be seen in sectoral productivity data. In the aggregate, Japanese workers were approximately 50% as productive as American workers in 1970. However, in industries such as automobiles, motorcycles, steel, and ship building, Japanese workers were between two and twenty times as productive as their American counterparts. The immediate conclusion is that other Japanese industries are extremely underproductive by world standards. In low-priority sectors such as paper, food processing, lumber, glass, footwear, and furniture, Japanese industry operates at a competitive disadvantage.

The two-tier structure extends to other dimensions of Japanese industry. The first tier is dominated by the large Zaibatsu or Sogo Shosha. The second tier includes hundreds of thousands of small firms, many of which act as suppliers to the first tier. Firms in the first tier comprise an unofficial business establishment, called *Zaikai* in Japan. This establishment dominates Japanese industry, but it is important to note that non-Zaikai firms can achieve notable success in Japan. Sony achieved its success without the benefit of preferential support from the Japanese system. Honda's entry into the automobile industry was vigorously opposed by the Japanese business establishment. Independent entrepreneurial ventures can and do succeed in Japan, but they do so without the direct, preferential support of the industrial policy apparatus. One key consideration for such firms is access to capital. Sony, for example, has a debt–capital ratio of less than 40%, which is extremely low by Japanese standards.

A principal benefit available to *Zaikai* firms in target sectors is privileged access to capital. We have noted that 13 large "city" banks dominate the Japanese banking industry. Each of these 13 banks also serves as the official or unofficial financial center for one or more of the dominant Zaibatsu groups (Mitsui, Mitsubishi, Sumitomo, etc.). This high degree of concentration would be unacceptable by American standards. It is also potentially restrictive of growth and innovation. Somehow, although Japanese capital allocation is closely tied to the outcome of the indicative planning process, the system is flexible enough to permit the development of successful entrepreneurial ventures such as Sony and Honda.

The Japanese economic system is structured to provide substantial support to its industry. Capital and labor markets, government policies and programs, and management philosophies all support the same objective of international industrial expansion. This powerful combination of forces has already proven effective in a variety of industries, and its momentum is unchecked.

REFERENCES AND NOTES

1. Foreign borrowing in Japan is rising rapidly to a total of $45 billion in 1980, but a large share of this total is from foreign affiliates of Japanese parent firms.
2. *Economic Statistics Annual,* Research and Statistics Department, Bank of Japan, March 1982, pp. 213–216.

3. Japanese corporations fund statutory health, pension, unemployment, and workers' compensation programs similar to their U.S. counterparts. However, nonstatutory worker benefits, especially housing, medical, food, and pension contributions, exceed statutory payments by 124%. From *Wages in Japan and the United States*, Ministry of Labor, Japan, and the U.S. Department of Labor (Washington: Government Printing Office, 1966).

4. For corporate profits, see: U.S. Department of Commerce, *Survey of Current Business*, April 1982, Table 6.20.; for transfer payments, see: Office of Management and Budget, *The Budget of the U.S. Government*, (Washington: Government Printing Office, 1982). This total includes retirement, disability, and unemployment insurance payments, public assistance payments, health care payments, veterans' benefits, and training and social services programs.

5. Profits data from *Japan Statistical Yearbook*, 1981, pp. 330–331. Federal payments data from *Economic Statistics Annual*, Bank of Japan, March 1982, p. 215; *Japan Statistical Yearbook*, 1981, pp. 358, 540.

6. Japanese welfare levels have been discussed widely. Certain data suggest that a great differential exists between Japan and other industrial nations in some areas of welfare. Suicide rates among elderly people in Japan are as much as 10 times higher than rates in other OECD nations. (Naomi Maruo, "The Level and Living and Welfare in Japan Re-Examined," *Japanese Economic Studies*, Fall 1979, Table 8.)

Housing quality is vastly inferior to Western standards. Only 31.4% of Japan's homes had flush toilets in 1973, compared to over 90% in other OECD countries. (*International Economic Statistics*, Economic Planning Agency, 1977) Other indicators appear in Hugh Patrick and Henry Rosovsky, "Japanese Economic Performance," in Patrick and Rosovsky (eds.), *Asia's New Giant* (Washington: Brookings, 1976).

Pensions are so inadequate that over three-quarters of retired workers take jobs at much lower pay and poorer working conditions in small second-tier companies. Signif-

icant private costs are incurred to keep the public welfare burden low. One view of this facet of the Japanese system is presented in E. van Helvoort, *The Japanese Working Man: What Choice? What Reward?* (Vancouver: University of British Columbia Press, 1979).
7. *OECD Economic Surveys: Japan, 1981* (Paris: OECD, 1981); *The Development of Industrial Relations Systems* (Paris: OECD, 1977).
Not only are benefits less secure in smaller firms, but they are also less substantial. The lump-sum retirement benefit paid to an average production worker with forty years of service varies sharply with the size of the company.

Size of Company	Lump Sum Payment (1978)
30–99 employees	$17,705.00
100–299 employees	$20,000.00
300–999 employees	$30,164.00

SOURCE. E. Van Helvoort, *The Japanese Working Man.*

One can only assume that pension benefits in very small companies are at most half as great as those in very large firms.
8. Foreign borrowers floated $1.1 billion in yen-denominated bonds in Japan in 1980, up from $90 million in 1975. Simultaneously, Japanese firms and agencies floated $3.7 billion in foreign currency bonds outside of Japan. Japanese capital markets have witnessed a dramatic increase in the inflow of foreign funds. Foreign investment in Japanese securities totaled $12 billion in 1980 alone. At the bank debt level, nonresidents borrowed $10.1 billion from Japanese banks in 1980, up from $1.5 billion in 1975. However, a large percentage of this total is to foreign affiliates of Japanese corporations.
9. *Economic Survey of Japan* (Tokyo: Economic Planning Agency, 1981), pp. 223–225; *International Finance Bureau Report*, Ministry of Finance, 1981.9. Housing mortgage debt outstanding in the United States totaled $1,018,742 million in 1981, a net increase of $58.15 billion over 1980. *Federal Reserve Bulletin*, March 1982, Table 155.

Outstanding housing loans by all banks and by the national Housing Loan Corporation in Japan totaled $113,020,000 million at the end of 1980. *Economic Statistics Annual,* March 1982, Bank of Japan, pp. 99, 145.

However, it should be noted that total investment in housing in Japan is much greater than this figure. Mills and Ohta estimate that commercial banks and the Housing Loan Corporation finance only 21% of the total value of housing purchases in Japan. The remainder is funded privately; 55.7% from personal savings, 15.2% from employer loans, and 5.1% by loans from relatives.

(E. S. Mills and K. Ohta, "Urbanization and Urban Problems," in Patrick and Rosovsky, *Asia's New Giant*).

10. For an excellent discussion of Japanese labor relations during this period, see: S. B. Levine, *Industrial Relations in Postwar Japan* (Urbana: U. of Illinois Press, 1958); Walter Galenson and Konosuke Odaha, "The Japanese Labor Market," in Hugh Patrick and Henry Rosovsky, *Asia's New Giant.*

11. R. Evans, Jr., *The Labor Economics of Japan and the United States* (New York: Praeger, 1971).

12. *The Development of Industrial Relations Systems; Some Implications of Japanese Experience* (Paris: OECD, 1977).

13. For a similar discussion of the nature and composition of small-group activities within the Nippon Steel Corporation see: *Productivity and Quality Control* (Tokyo: JETRO, 1980), pp. 19–22.

14. Scanlon Plan programs were widely used in the United States prior to World War II. See F. G. Lesieur (ed.), *The Scanlon Plan: A Frontier in Labor–Management Cooperation* (New York: John Wiley & Sons, 1958).

15. Quality circles have been adopted by over 400 U.S. firms. For example, see F. K. Plous, "The Quality Circle Concept: Growing by Leaps and Bounds," *World of Work Report,* April 1981.

However, R. E. Cole notes that "most of the experiences of these (U.S.) companies have been quite shallow. Thus it would be premature to make assessments as to their suitability to the American Environment."

See R. E. Cole, "QC Warning," *World of Work Report,* July 1981.

The ability of Japanese firms to apply small-group systems successfully in the United States is also subject to debate. Johnson and Ouchi found that Japanese plants in the United States were more efficient than similar U.S.-owned plants. They attributed the difference partially to Japanese labor relations systems. See R. Johnson and
W. Ouchi, "Made in America under Japanese Management," *Harvard Business Review*, September–October 1974. Later studies show that subsidiaries often fail to implement Japanese systems successfully.
See: W. Ouchi, "Success and Failure of Japanese Subsidiaries in the U.S.," *Columbia Journal of World Business*, Spring 1977; "Japan's U.S. Plants Go Union," *Business Week*, Oct. 5, 1981, pp. 70–76.

16. I. C. Magaziner and T. H. Hout, *Japanese Industrial Policy.*
17. Yoshi Tsurumi, *The Japanese Are Coming* (Cambridge: Ballinger, 1977); E. F. Vogel, "Guided Free Enterprise in Japan," *Harvard Business Review*, May–June 1978.
W. V. Rapp, "Japan's Industrial Policy" in Isaiah Frank (ed.), *The Japanese Economy in International Perspective* (Baltimore: Johns Hopkins Press, 1975).
For a countervailing opinion, see Philip Tresize and Yukio Suzuki, "Politics, Government and Economic Growth in Japan," in Patrick and Rosovsky (eds.), *Asia's New Giant.*

3

The U.S. Response
(1959–1979)

Our strategy was very simple. Whenever we hit mush, we pushed on.

V. I. Lenin

Competition between U.S. and Japanese firms has been highly one-sided in recent years. While American firms find it difficult to establish markets in Japan, Japanese efforts to penetrate American markets appear to have met little stiff resistance. This stems partially from careful selection of sectors and entry strategies by Japanese firms, and partially from the lack of a vigorous response by American firms. The absence of effective responses has led many to conclude that the United States is losing its industrial vigor and competitiveness.

A variety of statistics indicates that a decline in industrial strength has occurred in the United States. In the areas of manufacturing productivity, output, exports, and employment, U.S. industry has been a poor performer in the last decade.[1] Much has been written about the phenomenon. The reasons for this decline are usually associated with an ongoing evolution in social conditions and values, government roles and responsibilities, and managerial philosophies. Fundamental changes in social values have altered attitudes toward work, economic

63

growth, and industry. The government is often criticized for contributing to a decline in industrial competitiveness. Finally, changes in management philosophies and strategy within industry itself are cited as causes of the decline.[2] It is important to review past conditions and trends in these key areas before addressing current developments within the U.S. business environment. An observer describing conditions in the United States in 1979 might have focused on the following issues.

POSTINDUSTRIAL SOCIETY

Cornelius Vanderbilt, one of the great American industrialists, started his business career by developing a garbage transport monopoly in New York City. He once said, "I am doing what I do so that my son can become a lawyer and his son can become a historian." As American society has evolved along these lines, some would argue that it has moved further away from the sources of its strengths and prosperity.

This pattern is partially a matter of social choice. Noneconomic values and objectives have become more important in American society. Quality of life, recreation, leisure, and other intangible concerns have taken on greater significance in affluent postindustrial America. It seems that the status of the businessperson and industrialist has diminished accordingly. As Kenneth Boulding said, "Economic animals are all well and good, but I wouldn't want my daughter to marry one." The United States has become more civilized. Unfortunately, much of recorded history suggests that more "civilized" societies will be overtaken by those which are less so.

If progress toward a postindustrial state is used as the measure of a nation's achievement, the United States is a more advanced society than Japan. Industry, especially manufacturing, is not as important in the United States as it once was. The manufacturing sector in the United

States accounts for only one-quarter of Gross National Product today and that percentage is steadily shrinking over time. Success in the manufacturing sector is the primary focus and thrust of Japanese society. The industry of the Japanese work force, as seen in the Musashi example, is unparalleled. These differences in fundamental social values are reflected in education, work, and career patterns, and especially in the role of government. Changes in fundamental social values and objectives in the United States have translated into new roles and responsibilities for government.

THE ROLE OF GOVERNMENT

The success of Japanese industry relative to U.S. industry is often attributed primarily to the roles of their respective governments. Many would argue that the U.S. government handicaps rather than helps domestic industry in its competition with foreign rivals. The Japanese government protects and promotes its industry with single-minded zeal. Such dedication stands in dramatic contrast to the U.S. approach. Here, industrial performance is only one of many federal concerns. At least three others appear as important to U.S. policy makers as industrial performance: (1) America's standing in the military arena; (2) its role in the world of international politics and diplomacy; and (3) the performance of the domestic public welfare system. As a result of these additional concerns, support for industry is less focused in the United States than in Japan. Regardless of the degree of importance, the role of government vis-à-vis industry is also very different in these two countries. The economic roles and responsibilities of U.S. government have evolved along lines that have led to a reduction in industrial vigor. The extent of this trend becomes clear when one reviews the government's stated policies toward industry in the years immediately following World War II.

American Industrial Policy

The U.S. Council of Economic Advisors was created by an act of Congress in 1948. Although the Council's functions are solely advisory in nature, its creation symbolized a new role for government in managing the economy. The first report of the Council of Economic Advisors to the president, published in 1949, describes this new role in very moving terms.[3] The report details the basic beliefs and principles underlying the government's attitude toward business, and the philosophy guiding its involvement in the economic sector.

The report states that the first and foremost responsibility of government is to create an "environment conducive to business expansion." To accomplish this end, government will avoid direct controls, emphasize growth as opposed to redistribution, and attempt to maintain stability and balance in the economy through monetary and fiscal policies. Economic growth becomes the central objective of government policy.

> Once it is appreciated that general growth of the American economy can create within less than a generation a truly good standard of living for all, . . . the ancient conflict between social equity and economic incentives . . . is reduced to manageable proportions.

In accordance with this shift in philosophy, the report supports a move away from the use of specific controls and regulations and toward greater reliance on private enterprise as the engine of economic growth. The report argues for a limited governmental role in the economy, but stresses that "whatever the scope of government programs, [they] should be applied [with] principles of consistency and harmony." Further:

> Government's attitudes towards business are moving away from the purely negative or policing function and towards an affirmative or facilitative approach. The fiscal, credit,

monetary and other facilitative operations by which the
government may promote an environment conducive to
business expansion are at least as important as the traditional watchdog function.

This report represented an important declaration of
principles in the early postwar period. It evokes an image
of business and government working together to create
prosperity and material well-being in a free world. The
ensuing years, while filled with great success for the United
States, have tarnished this vision. Economic growth has
ceased, and economic stability has not been found even
in stagnation. The federal government has increasingly
directed its efforts at redistributing wealth rather than
promoting general growth. Massive direct controls and
regulations have been imposed on industry, and government policies vis-à-vis industry have not been applied with
consistency and harmony. The partnership between business and government has not been realized.

The federal government's role in the economy has grown
sharply since 1949. The federal budget accounted for 11%
of the GNP in 1949; today it accounts for 24% of the GNP.
In addition, its involvement in private industry has widened
dramatically in the form of regulations, controls, and direct
jurisdiction. Many argue that these controls have sapped
the vigor of American industry. What was once a dynamic
economic jungle has become the industrial equivalent of
a game preserve or zoo: a controlled, contained, and regulated environment. A caged animal, economic or otherwise, is no match for a wild animal. Nor is a caged animal
a match for a creature bred and trained for competition.

The shift in government policy away from the ideals
expounded in 1949 toward the realities of the present day
stems partially from changing social values. A desire to
curb business abuses and power and the assumption of
new governmental responsibilities have also contributed
to this trend.

The New Responsibilities of Government

The creation of the EPA, OSHA, favorable labor legislation, minimum wage standards, product safety laws, FDA regulations, and a variety of other controls has been stimulated by a desire to reduce business abuses. The concerns, abuses, and needs underlying these programs were unquestionably real. The unfair labor practices, unsafe products, unhealthy effluents, and unethical activities these acts were designed to limit were simply unjustifiable. The benefits of the programs have been great, but industry has borne significant costs to achieve them.

Often government activities have been stimulated largely by desires to appease new interests in the body politic. Many new programs, such as the Clean Air Act and recent nuclear policies, can be credited to vocal minority groups. Programs to provide broader welfare and consumer protection have had the general support of a larger constituency. These programs have also increased costs for industry.

Government curbing of business abuses extends into the world of business competition as well. The predatory and monopolistic activities of the robber baron era led to creation of antitrust laws in the nineteenth century. The philosophy that "big is bad" was an inherited part of government industrial policies after World War II. The largest and most successful U.S. companies found their freedom to compete constrained by these antitrust considerations. Antitrust concerns were not a new responsibility, although this function was pursued far more vigorously than it had been in the past. These concerns became important and growing responsibilities of government, but the most important new responsibility arose in the world of international diplomacy. The United States found itself the only power capable of filling the vacuum of world economic and political leadership after World War II.

Geopolitical Imperatives

The U.S. stood in 1949 in a uniquely powerful position. The dollar was the only currency with accepted international value. America was the sole source of capital for world reconstruction and development. U.S. technology in the forms of television, computers, the birth control pill, the jet plane, and nuclear power provided a fountain of new products to fuel economic growth. The United States played the primary role in shaping the postwar world economic and political order. One of the founding principles of that order was free trade. Another was open and free flow of capital. The United States opened its markets to foreign products and encouraged others to do the same. The bridges between markets were opened, bringing U.S., European, and Japanese and other firms into direct contact with each other on a large scale for the first time. Improvements in communications and transport encouraged firms to expand abroad at a unprecedented rate. Capital flowed out of the United States, stimulating growth and development in foreign countries. American corporations got the best of it almost everywhere—everywhere except Japan. Investment restrictions limited the U.S. industrial presence in Japan, and trade barriers limited exports into the market.

The bridge to Japan has been largely a one-way street. The U.S. government has been willing to accept and even encourage this state of affairs largely because of its role as diplomatic and military leader in the postwar world order. Reluctance to impose major trade restrictions on Japan stems from concern that such a precedent would damage the fragile free trade system, a system that has led to unprecedented world growth and prosperity. Reluctance to pressure Japan has also been reinforced because of its strategic political and military role. Japan provides a key diplomatic and military base in the Far East. Part of the price the United States pays for the continuation of that role is reflected in our Japanese trade policies.

All of these responsibilities and concerns have influenced the government's role in shaping the business environment in the United States. The resulting environment has had a negative impact on American industrial competitiveness.

INDUSTRY RESPONSE

The realities of social conditions and government policy have shaped the nature and competitiveness of U.S. industry. Corporate attitudes toward investment and competition have been molded by these conditions. To the extent that labor, regulatory, and antitrust considerations reduced investment and competitiveness, industry is blameless for its record against Japanese competitors. However, underlying changes in management philosophy and strategy have also reduced competitiveness. American industry is widely critized for its short-term financial perspective. That perspective has grown as individuals with finance backgrounds have assumed more and more senior management positions.[4] Emphasis on net present value analysis and a portfolio perspective on business strategy have opened the door for Japanese competition. What chould be easier than competing with a firm that is known to use strict ROI criteria for business evaluation and investment decisions? Only competing against a division formally acknowledged as a cash cow within such a company could be easier. It becomes an exercise similar to shooting ducks in a barrel for Japanese companies. Add to that a natural upgrading orientation as perfected by Alfred Sloan of General Motors and it can be seen that U.S. industry set itself up as an ideal target for Japanese competitors. These underlying changes in management attitudes, in addition to the social and regulatory environment, shaped corporate responses to Japanese competition.

There are several common themes which emerge from analysis of U.S. response patterns to Japanese competition. Although a wide range of options is available to managers, the critical choice lies between confrontation and avoidance. In many cases, the primary corporate response to a Japanese thrust in a marketplace has been to avoid direct confrontation. The reasons for this path of action can be related to the environment created by social values and government policies, but managerial preferences and philosophies also contribute.

Confrontation

For most U.S. companies, a decision to confront the competition directly will require major changes in operations. The company will need to increase product standardization, to increase automation in manufacturing, to reduce overhead costs, to increase the rationalization of manufacturing facilities, to become more price competitive, and of course, to pursue vigorously a program of cost reduction and quality improvement in all areas of activity.

Any effort to improve manufacturing efficiency will require the modernization or closing of existing facilities, and probably the development of new production sites. Large capital investments will be necessary to pursue such a program. American firms facing established or imminent Japanese competition may find raising funds to finance manufacturing modernization difficult. American capital markets legitimately view such companies as unattractive areas for investment. Even if funds are readily available, the relative cost of capital in Japan and the United States will work to the disadvantage of American firms. Other factors are also likely to leave American firms at a disadvantage in their efforts to improve manufacturing efficiency. Efforts to increase automation are likely to be met with labor resistance. Examples of this problem abound, but one of the most notable cases concerns the General Motors facility at Lordstown.

The GM Lordstown plant was opened in April 1966 to assemble Chevrolets. In 1970 the plant was retooled to produce the Vega—GM's new entry at the low end of the car market. The line was highly automated, and GM management expected the Vega to be a "zero-defect" car. Management also had high productivity and cost efficiency expectations. In attempts to meet productivity, output, and quality standards, the work force was selectively reduced during 1971 and 1972. The result was disaster:

> As 1971 turned into 1972, vehicles regularly began to come off the line with upholstery slashed, windshields smashed, wiring severed and bodies dented. It was possible to find engines which should have been assembled passing down the line as a neatly stacked pile of parts. The plant's repair bay, with space for 2,000 vehicles, frequently overflowed, halting production in the middle of a shift. Before 1971, about 300 worker grievances were filed per year. In 1971, the rate soared to 15,000. Absenteeism climbed to 7.4% and over 400 people were on discharge for disciplinary offenses.[5]

Labor relations can also limit efforts to close existing facilities and to centralize manufacturing. We have already seen an example of a company that chose to follow a strategy based on manufacturing rationalization in a highly competitive transportation equipment market. The firm eliminated a number of secondary facilities and centralized its production for axles, transmissions, and engines in single facilities designed to serve world markets. That company was International Harvester. International Harvester stands today on the brink of bankruptcy largely because its centralized manufacturing facilities were highly vulnerable to strikes. A United Auto Workers strike in 1979 effectively rendered the firm unable to deliver products to its markets.[6]

Another major effort to achieve cost reduction in many industries has been offshore sourcing of components and final products. This approach provides an immediate means of cost reduction, but to the extent that Japanese cost advantages are based on capital-intensive production strategies, an offshore production strategy based on the use of low-cost labor will be ineffective in competing with Japanese firms. Moreover, in many areas, Japanese firms already use offshore production sites as sources for highly labor-intensive components.[7]

Other means of achieving real cost reduction are old-fashioned value engineering, standardization of product lines, reduction in inventory holding levels, and elimination of various manufacturing, marketing, and administrative overhead costs. Reducing costs in all aspects of the firm's operations is critical regardless of the main thrust of the American firm's response. In many cases, however, the achievement of cost reduction objectives will not in itself be sufficient to maintain the American firm's position in the market. Even with cost structures similar to those of Japanese firms, American firms may be at a disadvantage because of different profitability requirements. Japanese firms simply have lower return-on-investment standards than American firms. Even with equal costs, the Japanese are willing to accept lower margins and profits.

Cost reduction alone cannot provide the competitive edge desired by American firms. Attempts to confront the competition will inevitably involve price reductions and, in many cases, a downgrading to more standardized, lower-priced products. Such an approach can result in the cannibalization of a more profitable existing line. The unattractive economics implicit in this approach lead most firms to consider other responses.

Even in the absence of significant cannibalization, many firms will prefer to avoid direct competition in the price-sensitive segments of the market. Margins are lowest in these segments, and the potential for ruinous rivalry is often great. One of the fundamental rules of management, especially in mature businesses, is to avoid price wars. This is one of the reasons that Japanese firms are successful in penetrating American markets.

It is easy to criticize American firms for their frequent unwillingness to confront Japanese competitors, but some solid arguments support this stance. It is difficult to compete effectively on the basis of price with Japanese companies. Moreover, the fact that the price war is inevitably fought in the American market means that most of the destruction is visited upon American firms. And, as we have seen, if the American defender does decide to engage in a price war, that firm will be at a financial disadvantage relative to its Japanese counterpart. American capital markets are reluctant to supply funds to firms engaged in price competition. And, finally, even if financing cost and availability are equal for the competing companies, financial leverage factors and labor, sourcing, and inventory costs, among others, will favor the Japanese competitor.

Avoidance

The avoidance response essentially focuses on various means of product differentiation. Rather than competing in the same segment directly on the basis of price and quality, many firms seek to differentiate their products from those of their Japanese rivals. A number of ways are available to differentiate a company's product. The upgrading of a product line is one such option. The emphasis in such a strategy is on premium products with extended features and performance, with a wider variety of models, or with additional options or greater size. The upgrading strategy can be based on radical or incremental product innovation. Another means of product differentiation is through promotion and advertising.

Product Differentiation. The premium product option has already been seen in the case of the automobile industry. American auto manufacturers' primary response to Japanese (and German) entry at the low end of the automobile market was continued upgrading of their product lines, an extension of product lines, and an increase in the number of options available to the consumer. Similar responses have been seen in other industries. Such an approach allows the firms in question to avoid direct confrontation with Japanese competitors. In some cases, the market may be willing to follow an upgrading strategy. An example of just this phenomenon can be found in the tire industry.

U.S. producers were facing significant competition from low-priced Japanese tire imports in the early 1970s. Japanese tire imports grew from virtually nothing to almost 10% of unit sales between 1965 and 1971. At the same time, competition in the premium segment was stimulated by the entry of the French tire company Michelin into the North American market. The U.S. industry's response to these threats was the introduction of new lines of very expensive radial tires, rather than low-priced products equivalent to those offered by Japanese companies.

The economics of such a strategy were undoubtedly superior to the economics of competing directly at the low end of the market. Demand for tires is highly inelastic in terms of units. Not only were the economics more attractive to American firms in this instance, but their competitive strength was far greater in the radial tire market than in the low-priced tire market. U.S. firms were able to retain over 90% of the domestic market for radial tires. Even more important, effective promotion of radial tires led many consumers to trade up from cheap Japanese imports to higher-quality radials. Radial tires now account for over 70% of all car and truck tires sold in the United States.[8] The Japanese share of the U.S. tire market shrank dramatically following introduction of radial tires by major U.S. tire companies in 1972. The Japanese tire companies continue to be active in the U.S. tire market, but their sales are largely associated with Japanese automobiles sold in the United States. Japanese firms have not yet established a presence in the U.S. radial tire market. The upgrading strategy, at least as it related to competition with Japanese rivals, was a successful response in the tire industry.

The introduction of the radial tire was effective because it encouraged upgrading based on a radical and obviously superior technology in a market in which product safety and performance were critically important. The risk of such an approach stems from potential consumer resistance to higher prices. Upgrading based on intangible product differentiation entails significant risks of consumer resistance. However, investment requirements for such strategies can be lower than those for radical innovation efforts because there is no need to revamp facilities or to change product lines dramatically.

Market Communications.   A common element in a product differentiation response—whether differentiation is fundamental or intangible—is advertising and promotion. Promotion skills are an important means of differentiating a product from those that compete on the basis of price. This area is one in which American firms possess great strengths. However, Japanese firms are also extremely effective in the areas of market research and market communication. In the motorcycle industry, Japanese firms and their agents identified a new user segment—the all-American youth as opposed to the Hell's Angel—and developed advertising themes designed to reach this market. Honda advertising campaigns made such statements as "You meet the nicest people on a Honda," and Honda was the first motorcycle advertised on television. In its first

Japanese Share of the United States Tire Market (1968–1975)

	1968	1969	1970	1971	1972	1973	1974	1975
Total U.S. sales (units in 000)	199,155	204,835	194,541	214,539	227,944	238,883	209,418	196,295
Total Japanese unit sales in the United States	216.2	492.8	1,081.4	1,896.4	1,849.1	1,305.0	1,038.7	692.4
Japanese market share	1.1%	2.4%	5.6%	8.8%	8.1%	5.5%	5.0%	3.5%

SOURCE: U.S. Department of Commerce.

five years of market penetration, Honda spent more than 10 times the amount of money that the existing domestic industry spent on advertising. Other Japanese motorcycle producers followed a similar strategy, although at lower levels of expenditure. Japanese firms have also spent heavily on advertising and market development in the automobile industry.

Despite the strength and skill of Japanese firms in advertising, many U.S. firms have tried to use this approach as a principal means of combating Japanese market penetration. Zenith, the leading producer of color television sets in the United States, relied heavily on advertising to differentiate its product in the 1970s. The Zenith ads emphasized the theme, "The quality goes in before the name goes on." These ads showed an American worker wiring a television chassis by hand, and emphasized that American craftsmanship resulted in a product of superior quality. Zenith's picture quality was in fact rated superior to Japanese sets by several consumer testing organizations, yet field defect rates for Japanese sets at that time were less than 25% of the defect rates for American producers. Two different concepts of quality are evident here—the Japanese concept of consistency, reliability and zero defect performance and the American concept of superior features and capabilities.

This is an important distinction. Perhaps the best example of successful product differentiation in the color television industry is that of Sony Corporation. Sony was able to achieve a premium image because its product uniquely combined both concepts of quality. Sony provides an interesting reference point for comparing American and Japanese industrial strategies. It is an excellent example of a successful non-Zaikai Japanese company. Sony was started in a basement by two entrepreneurs who got the name from the Latin *sonus* (sound), since they were selling audio equipment, and also from the American expression "sonny boy," because they viewed their venture as young and promising. The company is decidedly Western in orientation and operations, even to the point of maintaining a low debt–capital ratio. Sony did not employ the usual strategy of successful Japanese competitors. Instead, it sold a premium product priced far above existing market levels. It sold through specialty distributors, and did not produce in a single central facility in Japan. Sony began producing color television sets in the United States in 1971. Sony provides an interesting example of how American firms might compete against more traditional Japanese companies. Notably, Sony has been a technological leader in the color television industry.

Innovation. The most important means of providing some tangible difference in the product itself is through the kind of product innovation described for the tire industry. Continuing innovation can reduce the attractiveness of a sector to new entrants and thus can be used as a preemptive defense against foreign competition. Once competitors have entered a sector, innovation can also provide an effective response. However, it appears that Japanese firms have largely been able to match—and in some cases, outstrip—the technology of existing producers once they have entered a market. Their ability to respond to innovation appears to improve as their operations in an industry evolve. The television industry again provides an example of this phenomenon. Although U.S. firms were the original innovators in this industry, Japanese firms have long overtaken them. Solid-state circuitry was introduced in 1968 by Hitachi; the video cassette recorder was introduced in 1976 by Sony and Matsushita.[9]

The story that Japanese firms can not innovate is a myth. Their principal strategy involves entering industries in relatively mature segments, and focusing initially on process technology and value engineering, rather than product innovation. But as the Japanese strategy evolves in a particular industry, firms typically migrate into the premium product segments of the market in which product innovation becomes increasingly important. As Japanese activities in the consumer electronics and other industries suggest, product innovation is a growing element in Japanese success in certain world industries. One can expect that significant product innovations will be generated in Japan in years to come, and it may be that American firms in many more industries will find that strengths in innovation no longer provide a competitive advantage over Japanese rivals.

The End of the Line.   Another option for firms facing Japanese competition is diversification or even divestment. Although knowing when to withdraw is important, such a response is very unsatisfying. The line has to be drawn somewhere or there will be no place for American industry to compete. It is especially difficult for firms with narrow product lines to follow these options. How could General Motors or Ford or any other automobile producer completely divest itself of its automobile operations? Diversification is expensive and risky. Companies that are committed to a certain industry, such as Zenith, Harley-Davidson, Xerox, or Intel would find such an option very difficult to pursue.

Collaboration.   One popular approach used to avoid direct competition involves the negotiation of joint ventures or OEM arrangements with Japanese companies. At the most basic level, an OEM agreement involves an American firm's taking Japanese products and marketing them through its existing distribution channels. Examples of this approach exists in a number of industries. RCA Corporation markets a video cassette recorder produced by Matsushita. Chrysler markets automobiles manufactured by Mitsubishi. Ford and General Motors also market Japanese vehicles. Radio Shack markets a pocket computer manufactured by Sharp Corporation. Savin markets Ricoh copiers. The list of such arrangements is very long indeed.

A somewhat similar response is to form a joint venture with Japanese competitors. General Electric formed a television and video cassette recorder venture with Hitachi, for example. Such responses typically emphasize the role of the American firm in marketing and service and the role of the Japanese partner in manufacturing.

These approaches are equivalent to the notion of "If you can't beat 'em, join 'em." They permit the firm to avoid an immediate direct confrontation while conceding a part of the business to the new entrants. Such an approach entails a significant risk that Japanese firms will ultimately expand their activities into marketing, distribution, and service, just as they ultimately expand their activities into the premium segments of a market. Such a strategy can avoid short-term losses and costs, but may involve far greater risks and vulnerabilities in the long run. The risk is especially high if the American firm bases its strategy on its ability to deliver service to the consumer. In the television and automobile industries, Japanese producers have dramatically reduced if not eliminated the need for consumer service in many areas. In addition, Japanese activities in a number of industries have led to a shift in distribution patterns from specialty outlets to mass channels. Firms basing their strategy on distribution strengths will see their position erode over time.

LOBBYING AND LITIGATION

A common tactic used by U.S. industry when threatened by Japanese competition has been lobbying and litigation to gain government protection. Antidumping suits, antitrust suits, and other litigation and lobbying activities have been common in virtually all industries under attack. The success of these activities, however, has been limited.

Efforts to restrict Japanese imports in the color television industry were particularly extensive. The history of these activities provides an important perspective on broader aspects of the U.S. national response to Japanese competition. The American color television industry, led by Zenith, took several legal steps to restrict Japanese imports. An antidumping investigation was initiated in 1968. Support for this initiative appeared in 1971 when the United States Tariff Commission found that the U.S. television industry was being injured by imports of Japanese color television sets, and that such sets were being sold at less than fair value.[10] A second initiative was launched in 1970 when Zenith petitioned the U.S. Treasury Department to impose countervailing duties on Japanese color television imports. Under GATT and U.S. law, countervailing duties may be applied when a foreign competitor is proven to have received unfair export subsidies.

Investigation of the countervailing duty case was closed in 1976 when the Treasury Department issued a final determination stating that there was no cause for the imposition of countervailing duties against Japanese television imports. Zenith appealed the finding to the U.S. Customs Court, which unanimously upheld the company's position favoring countervailing duties. This Customs Court decision was later reversed in the Court of Customs Appeals. Finally, in 1978, the U.S. Supreme Court ruled that the Treasury Department's interpretaton had been correct, and that there was no basis for the imposition of countervailing duties.

Although both cases extended for years, the antidumping suit was far more complex and took longer to resolve than the countervailing duty case. Under existing U.S. legislation, responsibility for direction of antidumping suits rested with the Treasury Department. Acting on the 1968 complaint, the department announced in December 1970 that Japanese importers were guilty of dumping. Three months later, following the required Tariff Commission finding that domestic producers were being injured because of dumping activities, the Treasury Department began to assess fines. However, assessment of fines was halted less than a year later. One reason was the need to estimate the magnitude of dumping activity.[11]

Within the Treasury Department, the Customs Service was responsible for determining whether dumping was actually taking place and for calculating the extent of dumping activity. Determination of dumping is presumably a relatively simple exercise. Dumping is said to occur if a given product is sold at a lower price in a foreign market than it is sold in the exporter's home market. The Customs Service initiated an analysis of television prices in the United States and Japan in 1971 to compile data on prices for comparable Japanese television sets sold in the two countries.

For six years, the Customs Service investigators found it impossible to secure reliable information about the price of comparable Japanese television sets sold in the United States and Japan. They finally adopted a formula which subtracted value-added taxes in Japan from Japanese retail prices and used the resulting figure as a measure of Japanese prices for color television sets. Based on these price data, the Customs Service concluded that Japanese importers were liable for $400 million in dumping duties on television sets imported into the United States prior to 1977.

Japanese reaction to the Customs Service findings was swift and certain. Japanese government officials communicated to the U.S. State Department a vigorous protest of the methods used by the Customs Service to establish dumping duties. Japanese Minister Kawahara protested directly to the Treasury Department. Meetings between Japanese Ministry officials and U.S. Treasury officials were held. Shortly after these meetings, the Treasury Department, which was responsible for implementing the Customs Service findings, decided to delay the assessment of dumping penalties.

The dumping suit against Japanese importers has not yet been settled. The U.S. government has attempted to settle the case out of court, and the plaintiffs have agreed to pay a sum of $77 million to terminate the investigation. Sears, Roebuck and Company, the largest American distributor of Japanese color television imports, will pay $25 million of this total and other U.S. distributors will pay additional funds in concluding this case. This agreement has been blocked by Zenith's legal efforts, which hold that the fines to be paid are much too low. [12]

The legal and lobbying efforts of the U.S. color television industry had a limited impact on Japanese competitors. Similar efforts in other industries have also produced only limited successes. Where the United States has been successful in reducing imports, significant concessions have often been necessary. The textile industry provides an example.

Attempts to restrict Japanese textile imports began in the early 1960s and came to a head during the Nixon administration. President Nixon's agreement to limit Japanese textile imports was the culmination of several years of diplomatic activities. Three high-level economic missions headed by Secretary of Commerce Maurice Stans were dispatched to Japan in the summer of 1969 primarily to discuss this issue. Each of these missions proved unsuccessful, and Mr. Nixon was forced to involve himself personally in the negotiations. [13] Japanese Premier Eisaku Sato was invited to Washington. The *New York Times* reported the results of the two-day meeting as follows:

> On the first day, according to authoritative Japanese sources, the President conceded to Mr. Sato all the points he desired. The next day, however, the President took up economic problems, specifically textiles. . . .
>
> A grateful Mr. Sato apparently replied that he would do his best to resolve this problem. . . . The President accepted this statement as a commitment to restrict textile ship-

ment to the U.S. by a government to government agreement.[14]

Of course, no such agreement was recognized by the Japanese government. President Nixon's misinterpretation of Mr. Sato's statement is a classic American reaction to polite Japanese evasion. He is reported to have been so angered that he attempted to achieve his objective through new trade legislation, but that effort became mired in Congress. The textile agreement was ultimately achieved only because the U.S. Senate refused to ratify the treaty returning Okinawa to Japan until the Sato government "finally lived up to an informal understanding" to limit textile imports in exchange.[15] The treaty was then ratified in November 1971. Although the goal of restricting imports was achieved, it must be remembered that the textile industry was already a declining industry in Japan, one which was receiving reduced emphasis. Other instances in which the U.S. government was effective in coming to the support of a domestic industry under attack by Japanese competition are difficult to identify.

REASONS FOR U.S. GOVERNMENT RESPONSE

Throughout the 1960s and 1970s, the attitude of the U.S. government in responding to Japanese penetration of U.S. markets was essentially one of benign neglect. Efforts by American industry to secure the imposition of countervailing duties or restriction of imports through quotas or other devices were largely unsuccessful.

In analyzing why the U.S. government behaved in this manner, it is useful to consider the principles and the interest groups that support and benefit from such government behavior. On the one hand, the principle of free trade can be invoked to explain government actions in response to Japanese penetration of U.S. markets. The theory of comparative advantage argues that foreign industry, when it is more efficient than domestic industry, should capture a growing share of the domestic market, and vice versa. This philosophy is supported by significant industrial interests in the United States. The United States has been the world's largest exporter of manufactured goods. It is in the interest of these exporters that world trade be open and free and that the most efficient producers be granted unfettered access to world markets. U.S. commitment to free trade has been an underlying principle throughout the post–World War II era.

Another principle of U.S. policy that supports the position taken by the government in response to Japanese imports is that of free competition. The implicit belief that competition is good and increased competition is better leads to a policy that supports the presence of Japanese competitors in the U.S. market. Consumers have benefited greatly from this policy.

Consumer response to Japanese activities in the U.S. market has been predictably positive. The United States is a consumer society, and consumers benefit tremendously from Japanese presence in a marketplace. In every market the Japanese have entered, their activities have led to improved product quality, reduced service requirements, and increased value. Although Japanese products were initially viewed as inferior to American products, their reputation among consumers has obviously changed completely in recent years. As it is, Japanese industry is the single most powerful and positive force for industrial progress in the modern world. Japanese firms have reduced waste and inefficiency, have been more responsive to consumer needs and wants, and have developed means of improving product reliability and durability in such a way that economic efficiency in a global sense has been vastly heightened because of their activities. What level of product quality and value would be available today in the automobile market if Japanese firms were not present? What wage and price levels would have existed? This perspective must be considered.

No matter how attractive these benefits appear, however, it must be remembered that costs also are involved in permitting Japanese entry into U.S. markets. The costs in terms of unemployment, reduced profitability, and, in many cases, bankruptcy, are significant. There were once over 25 American producers of color television sets. Today there are 14, and 11 are owned by foreign companies.[16] In the steel industry, plant closings, dramatic losses, and reduced employment have been a way of life in the 1970s. In the automobile industry, there have been huge losses, plant closings, unemployment, and potential bankruptcies. U.S. government responses to Japanese competition suggest that the government believes that the benefits of Japanese presence in the U.S. market exceed the costs. But do they?

Government Roles in Japan and the United States

The governments of Japan and the United States have many basic differences in attitudes and policies. Let us begin with several of the most obvious contrasts. Japan exhibits a one-sided belief in free trade. Whereas the United States has been dedicated to a policy of free trade in the post–World War II years, Japan has been relatively reluctant to open its market to imports. On the issue of antitrust policy, very different approaches appear in the two countries. American policies have sought to reduce the concentration of economic power in industry and to increase competition within domestic markets, whereas Japanese policies are primarily concerned with the competitiveness of Japanese industry in world markets. In Japan the government has actively promoted the concentration of industrial power. Where cooperation and collaboration between firms in an industry are prohibited in the United States, the Japanese government actively encourages firms in the same industry to work together to share resources and to cooperate where it serves the national interest. Over 200 government-sponsored cartels are operating at present in Japan. Such policies are stimulated by the need to achieve the necessary economies of scale and manufacturing efficiency that are the backbone of Japanese competitiveness in world markets.

Let us consider the role of the consumer in these two countries. Japan and the United States differ greatly in their approach to the fundamental choice between consumer benefits and industrial security. In Japan consumers subsidize industry and labor in virtually every aspect of their existence. There are many ways in which the consumer pays this subsidy. Consumers are almost forced to save because of the absence of public welfare systems and the unavailability of financing for housing and durable goods. Many products, especially food and housing, are far more expensive in Japan than abroad.

One specific aspect of this difference in orientation appears in the Japanese distribution system. The number of small "mom and pop" retail outlets in Japan rose by approximately 300,000 units between 1964 and 1976. The number of wholesalers increased by over 100,000 between 1970 and 1979.[17] Japan is the only industrialized country to exhibit increased fragmentation of distribution channels. The result, of course, is reduced efficiency and higher prices for consumers. Yet this trend can be looked upon favorably by public officials, because it offers a vehicle for absorbing unemployment, makes Japanese markets less vulnerable to import penetration, and creates a large, pro-business political constituency. The price, in the form of an indirect tax, is paid by the Japanese consumer. Foreign exchange policies in these two countries also reveal important differences in government attitudes. The U.S. dollar was highly overvalued through most of the 1960s and 1970s. The Japanese yen was greatly undervalued during much of this period. U.S. consumers benefited greatly from cheap imports, but industry and labor paid a great price in terms of reduced domestic and foreign sales. The reverse was true in Japan.

Other aspects of national policies also reveal sharp contrasts between these two countries. The unity of business, labor, and government in Japan appears remarkable by Western standards, where a traditional adversary relationship has existed between business and government and business and labor. The role of government in capital markets is also quite different in the two countries. In Japan, a formal industrial policy influences the allocation of capital to industry, and the Ministry of Finance exerts administrative guidance within the banking system. In the United States, the government plays only an indirect role in determining which industries receive capital. When the government does intervene in the capital markets, it tends to be in rescue operations such as the Lockheed and Chrysler cases. Japanese public funding efforts, such as those financed by the Japan Development Bank, favor larger and future-oriented businesses. Public funding in the United States favors smaller and, in some cases, obsolete companies and industries.

Japanese capital markets provide a key source of support for formally identified target sectors. In the United States, target sectors are not formally defined. There is, however, at least one excellent example of a sector which has been defined, structured, and supported by the government. This example is NASA. The NASA program provides the best vehicle for examining national objectives and strategies in the United States.

The objectives behind NASA were not economic. The program was not concerned with balance of payments, economic growth, or employment objectives. The primary goal of the NASA effort was to contribute to the aim of achieving and maintaining a position of world leadership in technology, science, and military endeavors. These goals are part of a larger geopolitical effort that has driven U.S. policy since World War II.

An understanding of this effort is critical if we are to explain U.S. government policies toward Japanese industrial activities in the U.S. market. The United States has been very concerned about the political stability of the Far East since the end of World War II. The United States has been consistently willing to accept economic and human costs in order to promote political stability in the region. This perspective more than any other explains U.S. policy toward Japanese competition. By promoting Japanese industrial development, the United States could strengthen its greatest ally in the Far East, ensure regional stability, and maintain the existing geopolitical structure in the area. U.S. industry and labor paid a high price, but these objectives have been met.

As can be seen, the objectives of the American and Japanese governments have been very different during the last two decades. The Japanese system is completely dedicated to economic objectives. In the American system, economic objectives are far less important than political, diplomatic, and military objectives. The results of this difference are quite clear in the industrial arena.

The color television industry again provides an extreme example. In the course of 15 years, Japanese firms effectively came to dominate an industry pioneered by Americans. This industry not long ago was one of the most profitable, dynamic, and fast-growing industries in the United States. Although 15 years can be viewed as a long time in terms of industrial strategies, consider that an average Japanese manager could conceivably execute three similar strategies in the course of his career.

The reasons for such Japanese successes are fundamentally related to their ability to deliver a higher quality product at a lower price. Their success in U.S. markets is also fundamentally related to the responses of U.S.

competitors and the U.S. government. The industry's response to Japanese competition was ineffective. Failure to focus on manufacturing efficiency, product reliability, and world opportunities and threats contributed much to the industry's demise. Those firms that did survive—Zenith, RCA, and General Electric—have ceded world leadership in this industry to foreign rivals. A similar fate may lie ahead for the information processing industry.

REFERENCES AND NOTES

1. See for example: B. G. Malkiel, "Productivity—The Problem Behind the Headlines," *Harvard Business Review*, May–June 1979, p. 81; P. Capdevielle et al., "International Trends in Productivity and Labor Costs," *Monthly Labor Review*, December 1982, pp. 3–14.

    Data on comparative productivity, growth, export and employment performance can be found in *International Economic Indicators*, a quarterly publication of the U.S. Department of Commerce; in *OECD Economic Outlook*, an annual publication of the OECD; the *International Financial Statistics Yearbook* of the International Monetary Fund. See also *U.S. Industrial Outlook 1983* (Washington: Department of Commerce, U.S. Government Printing Office, 1983).

2. Some of the recent publications emphasizing these themes include: R. H. Hayes and W. J. Abernathy, "Managing Our Way to Economic Decline," *Harvard Business Review*, July–August 1980, pp. 67–77; R. B. Reich, "The Next American Frontier," *Atlantic Monthly*, March 1983, pp. 43–58; I. C. Magaziner and R. B. Reich, *Minding America's Business* (New York: Harcourt Brace Jovanovich, 1982); W. J. Abernathy, K. B. Clark, and A. M. Kantrow, *Industrial Renaissance* (New York: Basic Books, 1983).

3. See "Free Enterprise and Free Government and Trends in Government's Attitude Toward Business" in *Report of the*

U.S. Council of Economic Advisors (Washington: Government Printing Office, 1949) Sections I and II.

4. See Reich, op. cit., page 58; Hayes and Abernathy, op. cit., p. 74.

5. J. Child, "The Myth of Lordstown," *Management Today,* October 1978, pp. 80–84.

6. "The Strike That Rained on Archie McCardell's Parade," *Fortune,* May 19, 1981, pp. 91–99; "International Harvester: When Cost-Cutting Threatens the Future," *Business Week,* February 11, 1980, pp. 98–99.

7. The offshore activities of Japanese firms were first documented in detail by M. Y. Yoshino in *Japan's Multinational Enterprises* (Cambridge: Harvard University Press, 1976); and "The Multinational Spread of Japanese Manufacturing Investment Since World War II," *Business History Review,* Autumn, 1974. See also Y. Tsurumi, *The Japanese are Coming* (Cambridge: Ballinger, 1977).

8. For details on the market size and share of radial tires, see: "Less Means More at Firestone," *Fortune,* October 20, 1980, p. 115; "Goodyear," *Business Week,* July 12, 1982, p. 86.

9. "Backing Off Basics: Firms Stress Product Developing, Cut Research," *Wall Street Journal,* October 18, 1977, pp. 1, 36.

10. The Zenith account of and perspective on these events are presented in: J. J. Nevin, "Can the U.S. Survive Our Japanese Trade Policy?," *Harvard Business Review,* September–October, 1978, pp. 165–177. Another account appears in: "Zenith Radio Corporation versus the United States," Harvard Business School, ICCH 9-382-128.

11. Other reasons for the termination of fines were raised by John Nevin, President of Zenith, in a 1977 interview with *Forbes* magazine. He said: "There are two leading rumors. First, that the Japanese made an enormous campaign contribution to Nixon through Stans; but no one is going to track that one down. Second, that Nixon was having trouble in the south, and traded off textile protection at the expense of U.S. TV makers." *Forbes,* May 14, 1978, p. 69.

12. *Wall Street Journal*, April 29, 1980, p. 16.

13. *New York Times*, May 11, 1969, p. 6; July 31, 1969, p. 9; October 8, 1969, p. 71.

14. B. R. Scott, J. R. Rosenblum, and A. T. Sproat, *Case Studies in Political Economy:* Japan 1854–1977 (Boston: Division of Research, Harvard Business School, 1980).

15. *New York Times*, October 16, 1971, p. 1.

16. Japanese producers of color televisions in the United States are Matsushita (Motorola, Quasar, and Panasonic), Sony, Sanyo, Sharp, Mitsubishi, Hitachi, and Toshiba.

17. There were 1,673,000 retailers in Japan in 1979. A 1977 survey for the United States estimated that 1,855,000 retailers were in operation. "Japan: A Nation of Wholesalers," *The Economist*, September 19, 1981, pp. 88–90. M. Kanabayeshi, in P. R. Cateora and J. M. Hess (eds), *International Marketing* (Homewood, Ill.: Irwin, 1979), pp. 606–610.

II

The Information Technology Sector

4

The Seductive Sector

> *Everybody wants to get
> into the act.*
>
> Jimmy Durante

Worldwide sales in the computer and communications equipment market exceeded $100 billion in 1982. Growth rates for these markets as a whole are expected to continue at 15 to 20% per year for the forseeable future. At that rate, total sales would exceed $1.5 trillion in 1999. The size and growth of this market make it extremely attractive, but several other characteristics are even more important to Japan.

The objectives of maximizing a positive balance of payments and value added per worker have driven industrial policy and virtually every aspect of life in postwar Japan. The information technology sector offers a unique opportunity to pursue these objectives. Import requirements are minimal, and the value-added content is very high in this sector. Energy input requirements are uniquely low. With extremely attractive characteristics on each of these fundamental criteria, it is only to be expected that this sector should become the focus of Japanese industrial policy.

It would be misleading, however, to attribute Japanese interest solely or even principally to economic motives.

This sector offers far more than an opportunity to upgrade the activities of the Japanese economy. It can contribute to a more important goal: a national determination to achieve a position of world prominence, prestige, and leadership. Activities in the automobile and consumer electronics industries alone will not permit Japan to achieve such a position. Only two nonmilitary sectors hold such potential: energy and information processing. The first holds little promise for Japan. Only by dominating the information processing sector can Japan hope to achieve a position of world leadership through industrial activities.

The commitment of the Japanese government and industry to expansion in the information technology sector is complete. The economic attractiveness of the sector, given its size, value-added intensity, and minimal raw material import requirements, provides sufficient reason for this commitment. Its strategic importance in world industrial and social development provides a more important source of commitment. This industry is the sole vehicle available to launch Japan into a position of world leadership—a position that has been the focus of national efforts since Japan became part of the West in the nineteenth century. We can expect the Japanese system to pursue this industry with unprecedented dedication and single-mindedness.

Japanese firms will need to make unprecedented efforts to succeed in this sector, because it is quite different from others in which they have succeeded. Most segments of the information processing industry do not exhibit the characteristics generally associated with the automobile, motorcycle, or consumer electronics industries, for example. The mainframe computer segment, which has long been viewed as the primary focus of Japanese activities in the information processing industry, exhibits very high margins, low unit volume, low price sensitivity, low product standardization, and lacks mass distribution channels. All of these factors suggest that traditional Japanese industrial strategy will be less effective and applicable in the traditional computer industry.

Several other characteristics also suggest that the information technology sector will be less accessible to Japanese competitors than previous areas of activity. This industry exhibits rapid and frequent technological change, which limits potential product standardization and capital intensity in manufacturing. The sales and distribution process in most market segments requires a direct sales force and field installation, service, and maintenance abilities. A very high level of language skills is needed for software development, documentation, and customer service. Users of information processing equipment have very high switching costs because of fixed software and training expenses. The result is a high level of vendor loyalty. Moreover, the firms in this industry have been extremely sensitive to user needs. In contrast to the automobile industry, for example, the computer industry has a long history of improvements in price, performance, and other dimensions of product quality.

Key segments of the information processing industry are dominated by massive established companies. IBM's profits in 1982 exceeded the total computer sales of the six leading Japanese firms, and ATT is even larger. IBM and ATT are very different from the leading firms in other industries the Japanese have pursued. ATT has operated in a regulated environment with unique competitive conditions. The company has a progressive, long-term view of its mission, and it is not driven by conventional profit maximization objectives, since its profits have been determined as a percentage of capital employed. IBM is a non-unionized company with operations throughout the world. It has the largest installed base of computers in the Japanese market. Other leading U.S. computer makers are also very active in Japan. These activities provide a source of information about Japanese rivals, and also limit their ability to use the domestic market to subsidize foreign

Table 7   Industry Profitability in the United States and Japan

Industries	Profit to Total Assets			
	1977		1978	
	United States	Japan	United States	Japan
Average for all manufacturing industries	7.08%	1.80%	7.36%	2.12%
Office machinery	10.13	4.97	11.48	5.44
Computer equipment	12.91	2.39	14.31	2.47
Electronic components	5.85	7.72	6.80	7.83

SOURCE. *Sekai no Kigyo no Keiei Bunseki*, Industrial Policy Bureau, MITI, Tokyo, 1980, p. 22.

sales of information processing equipment. This presence reduces the domestic profitability of Japanese companies. The importance of this phenomenon might be seen in the data in Table 7. In the electronic components industry, where Japanese producers control virtually the entire domestic market, the Japanese industry is significantly more profitable than the U.S. industry. By contrast, the Japanese computer industry is significantly less profitable—in fact, about 15% as profitable as the American computer industry. A presence in Japan will help firms to anticipate Japanese activities in this industry. Lessons learned from other industries can also be used to prepare for Japanese competition. With forewarning and the experience of other industries as a guide, established American firms can make it more difficult to penetrate U.S. markets.

Another critical difference in this industry is the role of the U.S. government. The information processing industry is closely related to the military and defense efforts of the United States. Its defense applications provide an important competitive advantage for the United States in its rivalry with the Soviet Union. At the very least, federal research and development expenditures in defense-related areas will provide positive support to this industry.

One can also argue that economic factors are becoming increasingly important to U.S. policy makers. As the costs of maintaining a policy of free trade increase, reflected in domestic unemployment, bankruptcy, and stagnation, it can be envisioned that U.S. policy may well shift toward greater emphasis on economic objectives. This shift can already be seen in developments such as the imposition of import quotas in the steel and automobile industries, industries in which Japanese producers clearly have a comparative advantage. The combination of such economic and military pressures suggests that U.S. government policy in the information processing industry will be more potent and positive than it has been in other industries pursued by Japanese firms.

These fundamental business, market, and environmental conditions all pose formidable obstacles to Japanese penetration and dominance of the information technology sector. However, for the economic and strategic reasons already noted, the Japanese commitment to just this objective is total. The questions are: How will they seek to realize this objective? What strategy will they follow?

The initial issue is to determine which segments Japanese industry will concentrate on. Japanese firms have established operating bases in all major segments of the information technology sector. These bases vary in competitive strength, however, and the segments themselves differ in attractiveness. In order to assess the likely course of Japanese activities in this sector, we need first to assess the attractiveness of each of the major industry segments. Japanese strategic planners examine market, competitive, and operating conditions to determine which segments are most attractive. We can determine the likely focus of Japanese efforts by pursuing a similar analysis. The following sections will focus solely on market and industry characteristics in the United States and Europe. The Japanese market and industry will be examined in Chapter 5.

Three broad industries represent the core of the information technology sector: (1) components; (2) computers; and (3) communication equipment and services. Each can be broken down into a large number of segments. Within the component area the largest and most important segment is the semiconductor industry. Although semiconductors are sold to a wide variety of industries, over half of world output is used in computers and communications equipment, and the percentage is rising. Semiconductor technology plays such a vital role in these industries that this area occupies a central position in the information technology sector.

SEMICONDUCTORS

Japanese firms have already established themselves among the leaders in this industry (see Table 8). It is important to note, however, that two of the world's largest producers of semiconductors do not appear in the table. IBM, the world's largest semiconductor producer, manufactures solely for internal usage. Western Electric, with 1982 production valued at almost $400 million, also produces solely for internal use. General Electric and General Motors, among others, also have significant production for internal use.[1]

The semiconductor market can be broken into several broad segments. First, the distinction between discrete components and integrated circuits is important. Discrete components, primarily transistors and diodes, accounted for about one-third ($5.1 billion) of noncaptive world semiconductor sales of $16.5 billion in 1982. Integrated circuits (ICs) are rapidly replacing discrete components in

Table 8   Leading World Semiconductor Companies'
Sales (Discrete and Integrated Devices, 1982)

Company	Total ($ Million)
Motorola	1310
Texas Instruments	1227
Nippon Electric	1220
Hitachi	1000
Toshiba	810
National Semiconductor	690
Intel	610
Philips[a]	558
Fujitsu	475
Siemens[a]	420
Matsushita	340
Signetics (Philips)	384
Mitsubishi	380
Mostek	335
Advanced Micro Devices (Siemens)	282
Sanyo	260
AEG	196
Thomson-CSF	190
Sharp	155
SGS-ATES	150
Oki	125

SOURCE: Annual Reports, Hambrecht and Quist "The Japanese Semiconductor Industry."
[a]Not including U.S. affiliates.

many applications. ICs, or chips, can be placed into three
broad categories: logic chips, memory devices, and microprocessors. Logic chips contain circuits that process,
convert and direct electronic signals in predetermined
patterns. These circuits are designed to perform specified
tasks and functions upon "request" by an appropriate
electronic signal. Peripheral logic chips are also used to
manage interconnections between the various elements

of an electronic system. Memory chips store data and commands for processing activities. Microprocessors combine logic and memory functions on a single chip.

Logic Chips

Logic chips account for the largest segment of the IC market. These chips are silicon-based circuits which replace conventional circuits or entire circuit boards in electrical and electronic applications. The first logic chips produced in the late 1950s contained two or three circuit elements (resistors, transistors, diodes) in one circuit. By 1972, the logic chips in the IBM 370 contained 40 to 80 circuits per chip. Today a typical logic chip for a computer application will contain between 500 and 1500 circuits. Recent products have been announced that pack over 10,000 circuits on a single chip. Such continuing improvements at the microelectronics level are the driving force for progress in the broader information technology sector.

World sales of logic chips totaled about $6.3 billion in 1982. The greatest users of logic chips are the computer and communication industries, which together consume about 40% of total world output. Consumer products in the audio, video, watch, calculator, appliance, entertainment, and automobile sectors account for approximately a third of total logic chip use. The remainder of the market is accounted for largely by industrial and military equipment users.

Logic chips can be categorized as standard or custom products. Standard chips are produced for mass distribution to a wide range of users. Most chips on circuit boards fall into this category. Primary product categories in this segment include semiconductor switches, timers, amplifiers, comparators, regulators, converters, and interface devices. Such chips are usually purchased from independent electronics distributors. These distributors will sell over $5 billion worth of electronic components in 1983, mostly in passive components and standard integrated circuits for logic purposes.[2] World sales of standard integrated logic chips totaled about $5.6 billion in 1982.[3] Standard products dominate the semiconductor market because of several fundamental industry characteristics. The key success factor in semiconductor manufacturing is the yield of usable chips from a wafer of silicon. The delicacy of the process, which requires extremely precise tolerances, does not reward continuous adjustments of machinery to accommodate production of multiple devices. Fabrication lines are usually set up for large batches of one standard device. Producers invest in research to develop new, more complex devices suitable for wide application, and in plant and equipment designed for long production runs of standard components. The short life cycle of processing and fabrication equipment (three to five years and decreasing) further encourages high volume runs to achieve an adequate return on investment. These pressures have shaped competitive strategies which emphasize aggressive pricing of standardized components to maximize unit volume and minimize costs.

Despite these strong pressures towards standard products, the merchant market for custom chips is growing rapidly. This market totaled $700 million in 1982. Products in this category can be further defined as semicustom or full custom intregrated circuits. The two most important semicustom products are gate arrays and standard cell chips. A gate array chip consists of many preprocessed standard logic gates (a logic gate can be thought of as an on-off switch) that can be interconnected in any way according to customer preference. Gate array sales grew from $55 million in 1980 to $180 million in 1982. Standard cell chips are the silicon equivalent of a circuit board. Standard logic functions or cells are taken from a circuit library and placed in the desired location on a silicon chip. Standard cells are also growing rapidly, from $6 million in

1980 to $32 million in 1982. Sales of semicustom chips are forecast to grow at a rate in excess of 50% over the next five years.[4]

One of the most dynamic segments in the logic market is for full custom products.[5] These chips are fully unique for each application and user. By designing circuits precisely to user needs, significant space savings and processing efficiencies can be gained. Captive producers are extremely active in custom chip production. About 60% (or $1.8 billion) of all captive IC production is in custom chips. Nonetheless, merchant vendors are increasing their production of custom chips at a rapid rate. Consumer products, such as video games, personal computers, automobiles and appliances, and military applications have been the major uses of custom chips. However, many of the consumer product chips that were originally designed for a specific customer have become so widely used that they can now be considered standard logic chips. The nonproprietary consumer product chip market has essentially the same characteristics as the standard logic chip market. The original producer of such chips develops the circuit design in conjunction with the customer. Subsequent producers of these products operate exactly as they would in selling any standard logic chip.

The large existing semiconductor companies have tended to focus their activities in the standard chip market. Texas Instruments, Motorola, Intel, and National Semiconductor derive most of their logic sales from this market, but TI and Motorola have been active in the design and sale of high-volume consumer chips. A large number of new start-ups have appeared in the custom and semi-custom chip markets in the last year.

Despite the surge in chip usage by the auto industry and other consumer product areas, the greatest growth in demand for logic chips is in the computer and communications sector. This trend is particularly notable in Japan.

In 1979 consumer products used more than half of all the ICs produced in Japan. In 1983 these industries will consume only about 40% of all IC output.

Memory Chips

Memory products account for about one-third of the total IC market, on sales just over $3 billion in 1982. This market can be further segmented according to the type of process technology used in creating memory products and the type of memory product. The three main technologies are also the three principal processes used to produce logic chips. The three techniques are known as bipolar, MOS (metal oxide semiconductor), and complementary-MOS or C-MOS. The bipolar technique is the original process used to produce adjacent positive and negative charged areas in a silicon substrate. Current flowing from a positive "emitter" to a negative "collector," or vice versa, activates semiconductor circuits for logic or memory purposes. The MOS approach differs in the use of a "gate" between charged areas. When the current flow through the gate reaches threshold levels, the circuit switches on.[6]

MOS devices are superior to those produced by bipolar techniques in terms of density and power requirements—two critical performance criteria for semiconductors. MOS technology dominates the memory area, accounting for about 75% of all memory devices. C-MOS units may overtake the bipolar devices in 1983 as the second most popular technology base. C-MOS technology permits the use of a single charged area as both the emitter of one circuit and the collector for another, and thereby dramatically reduces power usage of the chip. C-MOS chips are particularly useful in battery powered applications. C-MOS memory chips have grown from sales under $100 million in 1980 to sales forecast in excess of $400 million in 1983.

The four principal types of memory products are RAMs, ROMs, PROMs, and EPROMs. The semiconductor memory

Table 9 Worldwide Unit Sales of Semiconductor RAM Memories, 1972–1982 (Millions of Units)

Type	1972	1973	1974	1975	1976	1977	1978	1979	1980	1981	1982
1k	2.5	7.0	11.5	19.0	14.5	7.0	6.0	4.0	0.0	0.0	C.0
4k	0.0	0.0	0.0	1.5	14.5	40.0	65.0	78.0	65.0	26.0	18.0
16k	0.0	0.0	0.0	0.0	0.0	1.0	6.5	2.40	79.0	252.0	22C.0
64k	0.0	0.0	0.0	0.0	0.0	0.0	0.0	0.0	0.2	9.0	61.0

SOURCE. Dataquest.

market originated in 1971 when Intel introduced its 1k random access memory (RAM) chip. A RAM differs from a ROM (read-only memory), the other principal memory product, in that the contents of the RAM chip can be written or changed by the user. The contents of a ROM are fixed, although it can be programmable (PROM) by the user. An erasable PROM (EPROM) has the characteristic of a RAM; but erasure requires special chemical or electrical treatment. The market for semiconductor memories has grown quickly since introduction of the RAM. Four successive generations of RAM memory products have been introduced in the last decade; each has exhibited dramatic reductions in cost per bit and each has surpassed its predecessor in unit sales.

The present market for memory chips is dominated by 16k RAMs, sales of which peaked in 1981 at about 250 million units. The next generation of 64k chips began to emerge in 1981 with unit sales approaching 10 million. Sales of these units in 1982 exceeded 60 million units.

Japanese activities in the 64k RAM segment have been widely publicized. Although IBM first began mass production of 64k chips for internal use in 1978, Fujitsu was the first firm to offer this product commercially in 1979. Aggressive capacity expansion has taken place since that time. Nineteen firms in the United States, Japan, and Europe now produce 64k RAMs. The most aggressive firms in this segment have been Japanese, but Motorola, Texas Instruments, and other U.S. producers have also been expanding capacity at a rapid rate.

One byproduct of this trend in capacity expansion is continued rapid reductions in memory prices. The average selling price for a 64k RAM in early 1981 was about $30 per unit. By the end of the year, average prices had fallen to about $5 per unit. Prices remained at that level through 1982. The price of a 16k RAM fell from $5.50 to $1 over this same period.

Acceleration of technology cycles for chips can be expected in the memory field because of competitive pressures. Nippon Electric and Hitachi initiated pilot production of 256k RAMs in the fall of 1983.[8] Japanese pressure on prices, capacity, and technology continues to be a driving force in this industry.

Microprocessors

The third main arena in the integrated circuit market is the microprocessor segment. Like the semiconductor memory, the microprocessor was first introduced by Intel in 1971. The microprocessor market is also presently entering its fourth generation. The first microprocessor, the Intel 4004, was developed for a now-defunct Japanese calculator company, Busicom Inc.[9] This 4-bit processor was seen as a potential standard replacement for a set of custom-made logic chips. Shortly thereafter, the potential of the microprocessor concept was greatly enhanced by three developments. First, the invention of the EPROM (erasable programmable read-only memory) permitted the user to customize and change processor logic structures. Second, the microprocessor was combined with memory capacity and input/output devices. The development of the "computer on a chip" occurred as these capacities were placed on the same chip as the microprocessor unit. Third, the development of the second-generation micro, the Intel 8008, permitted processing of 8-bit units—the length of a standard byte or processing unit in most data processing systems. By 1976 several dozen other companies had introduced 8-bit microprocessors. Although 4-bit units are widely used for games, toys, appliances, and other low-sophistication applications, the largest segment is in second-generation 8-bit units. The 8-bit segment accounted for about 40% of the total market in 1982.

The 16-bit segment is growing rapidly from $105 million in 1980 to $212 million in 1982. Microcomputer periph-

Table 10   Sales of Microprocessors and
Microcomputers ($ Million)

Size	1980	1981	1982(E)	1984(E)
4-bit	279.0	352.0	411.0	519.0
8-bit	358.8	426.6	480.1	596.3
16-bit	105.5	196.6	211.5	422.8
32-bit	0.0	0.0	3.7	200.0

SOURCE. Dataquest.

eral chips, used for input/output and other support functions, are also an important market segment, totaling $385 million in 1982.

The newest generation of 32-bit microprocessors was first introduced in 1981. The power of this fourth generation of microprocessors far surpasses that of the previous generation. The new Intel APX432, the first 32-bit microprocessor, has a computing power of two million instructions per second—equivalent to the capacity of the IBM 370 mainframe computer.

The microprocessor area is largely dominated by American producers, although Japanese firms are very active in the segment for consumer applications. Intel, Motorola, Texas Instruments, and Zilog are the leading producers of microprocessors. Japanese microprocessor products are either licensed from U.S. producers or derivatives of American models. American makers determine the standards, and Japanese and European producers serve as "second sources" for U.S. products. This practice, widespread in the industry, provides security to end users and also aids in international marketing efforts. Examples of formal second-sourcing arrangements for the present generation of 16-bit microprocessors appear in Table 11.

Microprocessors have been subject to the same relentless reduction in prices and improvement in performance

Table 11 16-Bit Microprocessors: Models and Manufacturers

Original Manufacturer, Model and Date of Introduction			
Motorola 6800 (1979)	Intel 8086 (1978)	National 1600 (1981)	Zilog Z8000 (1980)
	Other Suppliers		
Mostek (1982)	NEC (1980)	Fairchild (1983)	AMD (1982)
Signetics (1982)	AMD (1982)	Synertek (1983)	SGS-ATES (1982)
Rockwell (1982)	Fujitsu (1981)[a]	Eurotechnique (1983)	Sharp (1982)
Hitachi (1981)	Siemens (1982)		
Thomson-CSF (1982)	Harris (1982)		
Philips (1983)	Matra-Harris (1982)		
	Mitsubishi (1981)		

[a] Fujitsu produced the 8086 through reverse engineering procedures prior to receiving a license in 1981. The license involved no royalty payments, but committed Fujitsu to use the 8086 in a new generation of office equipment.

that mark the memory market. The price of the Intel 8088 has fallen from $32 in early 1981 to under $20 in early 1983, for example. As a result, sales volume for microprocessors is expected to grow from about 240 million units in 1981 to 450 million units in 1983.

Geographic Markets

The United States, Europe, and Japan account for about 90% of all semiconductor consumption. Both the United States and Japan are largely self-sufficient in terms of local production, with a bilateral trade flow that slightly favors Japan. The United States experienced a $36 million deficit in IC trade with Japan in 1981. The deficit jumped to over $300 million in 1982, however. Europe, in contrast, imports over half of its semiconductors. This import market is almost entirely dominated by American producers.[10]

American producers are rapidly increasing their production capacity in Europe. Texas Instruments operates six facilities in England, France, West Germany, Portugal, and Italy. Motorola has facilities in Toulouse, France, and East Kilbride, Scotland. National Semiconductor also has a facility in both France and Scotland. IBM, with major plants in Corbeil, France and Sindelfingen, West Germany, is the largest producer of ICs in Europe. In addition to these leading firms, several dozen U.S. electronics firms have established facilities in Ireland and Scotland under the industrial development assistance programs in those areas.

THE COMPUTER INDUSTRY

Worldwide sales of computer systems exceeded $75 billion in 1982. Within this market, a number of relatively distinct segments exist. The most basic distinction is in the size of the system. Computers range from personal computers

Table 12   Sales of Semiconductors by User, Area, and Year[a,b]

User	1978	1979	1980	1981	1982
United States					
Total semiconductors	3122.7	4295.4	5443.0	6690.2	7524.9
Discrete	971.2	1198.8	1213.0	1338.8	1322.4
Integrated circuits	2151.5	3096.6	4230.0	5351.4	5942.2
Europe					
Total semiconductors	2419.4	2887.4	3604	3900	4000
Discrete	1072.8	1121.1	1453.8	1700	1600
Integrated circuits	1336.8	1766.3	2150	2200	2400
Japan					
Total semiconductors	2587.9	2878.7	3676	4521	4973
Discrete	1216.3	1151.7	1269	1591	1353
Integrated circuits	1371.6	1727.0	2407	2930	3620

SOURCES. Semiconductor Industry Association 1980–1981 Yearbook. *Dataquest*, see *Financial Times*, "Electronic Components," April 5, 1982, Section III. MITI, see *Electronics*, January 13, 1982, pp. 121–152, Hambrecht and Quist, "The Japanese Semiconductor Industry," January 31, 1983.
[a]This table reflects sales in the merchant market only.
[b]Amounts are given in millions of dollars.

priced below $100 to supercomputers which cost over $10 million. These segments exhibit different competition, cost structures, customer bases, and channels of distribution but they also have many common characteristics. Competitors from several formerly distinct segments are converging rapidly. Yet, success factors remain unique in some segments. The most obvious example appears in the newest and most dynamic segment of the computer industry.

Microcomputers

The microcomputer industry can be traced directly to Intel's 1971 introduction of the microprocessor. The availability of low-priced microprocessors soon led to the development of a new type of small computer. The first of these computers were created by hobbyists who combined one of the new microprocessors with input/output and memory devices to produce crude but effective data processing systems. Soon, kits were being sold through direct mail ads in magazines such as *Popular Electronics*. These kits were purchased principally by a small group of professional and scientific users. Apple Computer Company and others began in this way.

The microcomputer market includes four broad user categories: business, scientific, education, and home. In addition, three broad product categories can be discerned. The low end of the personal computer market, in the $400-and-below segment, is dominated by Atari, Commodore, Texas Instrument, and Sinclair. Commodore's principal product, the VIC-20, sells for under $100 and is manufactured in Japan, the United States, and Europe. Annual sales exceeded 850,000 units in 1982, with Europe and Japan each accounting for 10 to 20% of total sales. Sinclair's low-end computer, manufactured by Timex, is priced at under $100, and it sold over 500,000 units in 1982. Atari also sold over 500,000 units in 1982; the Atari 400, its largest seller, retails below $200. Other principal competitors in this segment include Texas Instruments and Tandy, which offers an OEM version of Sharp's pocket computer that sold an estimated 260,000 units in 1982 in addition to its TRS models.

The second price segment of the personal computer market is that market developed by the Apple II and Tandy's

TRS-80. The Apple II, the grandfather of all microcomputers, had an installed base of about 700,000 units by the end of 1982 (Table 13). Products in this segment typically offer 32k to 64k RAM capacity plus disk storage of 200 to 300 kilobits, disk drives, a monochrome display, and a printer for under $3000.

While highly attractive, this segment is vulnerable to extension by companies in the lower tier of the microcomputer market. Commodore introduced its Commodore 64 in 1982. This model can run the software of both the Apple II and TRS-80 personal computers, claims to offer equivalent performance, and was initially priced at $595.[11] Atari's 800 model is priced at an equivalent level with similar features. Other low-priced competitors in this segment include companies like Franklin, which offers an imitation of the Apple II. In addition to increased penetration by low-priced products, more expensive machines are capturing a growing share of the microcomputer market. The most important is the IBM personal computer, which sold over 200,000 units in 1982 at an average price of about $3500.

The third tier of the microcomputer market includes systems generally selling for $3000 to $8000. These systems offer additional memory, greater CPU capacity

Table 13   Apple II Sales

Year	Units	Average Unit Value
1977	570	$1,358
1978	7,600	1,034
1979	35,100	1,364
1980	78,100	1,500
1981	192,000	1,806
1982	360,000	1,669

SOURCE. Rosen Electronics Letter, Apple Computer Company.

based on a more advanced microprocessor, a wider range of functions, including graphics and word processing capability, and more powerful printers and displays. Although Apple and Tandy have upgraded into this market, IBM and Hewlett-Packard have been the leaders in the market to date. DEC has introduced three units in this segment. Burroughs, NCR, and Savin each entered this market in 1981 as OEM distributors of a new desk-top computer made by Convergent Technology Corporation. Apple's Lisa work station is positioned at the high end of this segment.

New competitors have found it relatively easy to enter the personal computer market. The technology is not especially difficult; key components can be purchased from independent suppliers. Capital is required to fund product and market development, but venture capital money is readily available and the personal computer industry has remained a glamorous area. The largest barrier to entry appears to be access to distribution channels, especially scarce retail shelf space.

Distribution Channels

Distribution channels have evolved with the personal computer industry. Computer retail chains have expanded rapidly. The largest of these, Computerland, has over 250 outlets in the United States. Some nationwide department store chains, such as Macy's and Sears, have opened personal computer centers. Sears plans to open 55 such centers. Computer manufacturers compete vigorously for shelf space in these stores. A few manufacturers, including IBM, Xerox, and DEC, have their own stores, although their personal computers are also sold elsewhere. The IBM product centers sell only IBM products, while the Xerox stores carry several brands. Most stores carry no more than three or four brands, and many do not sell the full line of the manufacturers they do carry.

Retailers select the manufacturers they carry on several criteria. The profit margin they earn is one important factor. Retail margins range from 25% to over 50%. They rely heavily on the manufacturer for training materials, point of sales displays, brochures, cooperative advertising, and repair service. Some manufacturers devote a great deal of time and effort to dealer education and training. Both Apple and IBM require a prospective dealer to complete product training sessions before he or she becomes an authorized dealer. Availability of software and accessories is also important to dealers. Prospective customers usually approach a retailer with several applications in mind. If several software packages and hardware accessories are available for a certain computer, the dealer can offer more solutions and he or she will tend to prefer that system over a more limited one.

Service support from the manufacturer is important, because a salesperson can assure a customer that the computer will be repaired locally, and in a short time. Apple, for instance, offers service training to its dealers so they can fix most problems either while the customer waits or later that same day. If the problem is more severe, the dealer can send the computer to the local Apple service center, which has a one-day turnaround time. The dealer is authorized to loan a computer to a customer while his or her own machine is being repaired. Warranties are also considered important by dealers in their selling efforts. Most manufacturers offer a ninety-day warranty on all their products and will provide up to a one-year guarantee for an additional charge.

Personal computers are distributed through channels other than retail stores. Mail order accounts for a large share of the business. Apple, IBM, and TRS, three of the largest suppliers, do not authorize sales of their products through the mail. A large amount of software and peripheral equipment is sold through the mail, however. Another channel of distribution is the traditional direct sales force.

Some firms sell direct to large-volume accounts. Computer emporiums such as the Boston Computer Center (BOSCOM) are another new wave in personal computer distribution.

Role of Technology

While technical barriers to entry are relatively low, the personal computer business is nonetheless driven by developments in technology. Advances in microelectronics are the primary driving force behind the growth of the industry. Further advances will play a major role in the evolution of personal computers in the next decade as well. Advances in software will also exert a great influence on the direction of the industry.

Hardware advances are likely to occur in two areas: memory chips and microprocessors. Most microcomputers in 1982 use 16k RAM chips. However, high quality 64k RAM chips are available at low cost from American and Japanese suppliers. The first commercial-volume 256k RAM chip was introduced near the end of 1982. Availability of low-cost 256k RAM chips promises greater capabilities and price–performance standards for microcomputers. With such memory chips, manufacturers can utilize more of the memory addressing capability of microprocessors. Greater available memory permits more sophisticated and powerful software, faster execution time, and higher resolution graphics. Fewer chips also mean lower cost and higher reliability.

Advances in technology are not incorporated into personal computers immediately. The lead time from introduction of a new microprocessor until it is designed into a microcomputer appears to be three or more years. Motorola's 16-bit microprocessor introduced in 1979, the M6800, only appeared in personal computers in mid-1982. All the leading personal computers on the market in 1982 used 8-bit microprocessors.

Other hardware advances are directed at the human interface with computers, rather than at increasing computing power. For example, a device called the "mouse" allows the user to direct a cursor around the monitor screen by moving a hand-held control over a table top, and to give commands to the computer by pushing a single button. This device was first featured on the Xerox Star work station and is used in Apple's Lisa. Improvements in printers, terminals, and other input/output devices also are occurring rapidly.

Acceptance of the latest technology in the marketplace is constrained by the lead time required to utilize the previous cycle's products fully. Several years are required to develop peripheral hardware, accessories, and applications software to complement the hardware. The acquisition of this equipment and software represents significant investment, and therefore buyers are reluctant to replace that equipment quickly. This inertia tends to inhibit quantum leaps in microcomputer applications of the latest electronics technology. Machines based on the newest memory or microprocessor technology lack a broad base of software and other support.

Such constraints on the application of new technology were due largely to one element of software, the operating system. Operating systems, the control programs for the computer, are structured around specific microprocessors, as CP/M was for the Zilog Z80. CP/M (control program for microcomputers) is the most widely used operating system for personal computers. Introduced in 1975 by Digital Research, CP/M established an accessible industry standard, and thousands of applications have been written for it. As a result, the Zilog Z80 is the most widely used 8-bit microprocessor. Apple's DOS (disk operating system), Tandy's TRS-DOS, and Microsofts's MS-DOS for the IBM PC are other widely used operating systems. Their broad acceptance inhibits development of new systems, and encourages new entrants to build their systems around one of the accepted systems. As of late 1982, software could be written to be used only on one operating system. Translating programs to another operating system was expensive and time-consuming.

Software strategy is a key issue for all personal computer makers and users. Established companies and users have a large investment of proven software written around existing operating systems. At the same time, more powerful and sophisticated operating systems like ATT's UNIX are being developed. It is conceivable that a new operating system with the ability to run programs of the other systems might emerge. A microcomputer with this capability would contain several microprocessors and could support virtually any application program. In addition, all makers and users also have to consider the possibility that a specific operating system could come to dominate the personal computer market.

The potential for an operating system to gain such broad acceptance depends in part on who owns the rights to it. Apple's DOS is proprietary to Apple, and not available for license. CP/M and MS-DOS were written by software firms who had financial incentives to promote the use of their systems by hardware and software developers.

Technology and Competitive Strategies

Personal computer manufacturers could use several strategies to break into the personal computer market. One is to develop a machine with superior performance, using the latest technology. For example, the Fortune 32:16 uses the advanced Motorola M6800 microprocessor, a highly sophisticated operating system (XENIX, Microsoft's version of Bell Labs' UNIX), floppy disks that hold up to 800k, up to 1 megabyte of RAM, and sophisticated graphics. By contrast, the Apple III and IBM PC have slower processing, half the RAM, and lower disk storage. The success of such a strategy hinges on translating technical superiority into improved performance for the user. Superior performance can offset a manufacturer's lack of reputation, limited distribution, or small software base.

A company that excels in hardware engineering but lacks the resources to distribute its product widely could sell on an OEM (original equipment manufacturer) basis to systems marketers. Convergent Technologies markets its high-performance work stations this way through Burroughs and Honeywell, among others. OEM agreements are not limited to large mainframe makers. Hundreds of small specialized systems houses operate on this basis. By integrating and packaging available hardware, systems houses create and install customized turnkey products to user specifications. Sales to such agents offer an alternative approach to direct marketing. NEC and Sony, for example, have made major efforts to have their personal computers adopted by systems houses for use in specific applications such as hotel or accounting services.

Another approach to the market is based on production of a low-price imitation or "knockoff" of a successful computer. Franklin's Ace 100 is a knockoff of the Apple II; it looks like the Apple II and is compatible with most Apple II software and hardware accessories. Franklin's ads show a closeup of the Ace 100 keyboard with a shiny red apple perched on top. Its sales have grown despite limited distribution and ongoing lawsuits with Apple. Apple has many other imitators. Ads for the Pineapple have appeared in the United States, and Apple has fought the Lemon in Italy, the Orange in Asia and Australia, and the Apolo in Hong Kong. Such imitators require minimal research and development capabilities and no software development. Success depends on low price, permitted by low engineering costs, and an established base of software developed by someone else. Since such firms are often unable to support a dealer network, knockoffs are commonly distributed through the mail.

For most firms, compatibility with a major operating

system and software base is a key element in their strategy. Some firms have taken this strategy one step further by engineering two microprocessors into the system. These computers are known as dual processor systems. Typically, one processor is the Z80, which runs CP/M. Over 7000 software packages are available for machines that support CP/M. However, the Z80 is slower and can address less memory than newer 16-bit processors. The second processor is usually a faster chip such as Intel's 8086 or Motorola's M68000. While little software has been developed for these more advanced processors, dual processors allow the user to upgrade his or her computing capabilities as new software is published. In the meantime, the full line of software for CP/M can be used. This strategy is becoming increasingly popular, as it hedges against CP/M's becoming an industry standard, on the one hand, and against obsolescence of 8-bit systems on the other. The IBM personal computer, among others, has space for a second processor. The incremental cost of dual processors is small, less than $50 per unit, so it is seen as a powerful means of satisfying short- and longer-term needs.

Market Segments

The four main user segments in the personal computer industry are the business, home, science, and education markets. Business users have been the principal purchasers of medium- and high-priced microcomputer. These customers account for over 60% of the installed base for machines priced at more than $1000. The business segment of the personal computer industry can be further segmented as follows: stand-alone systems, and networked data processing systems and office work stations.

The Business Segment.   Stand-alone microcomputers are used both by small businesses and by individuals within larger organizations. Small business users are primarily interested in systems that can perform bookkeeping, order processing, payroll, inventory management, and other basic business functions. These users require a software base designed for these functions, and a fairly high level of training, service, and support. Microcomputers aimed at this segment must compete against small business systems such as IBM's systems 23, 34, 38, and 36.

Individuals in larger organizations often write their own programs and have access to internal expertise, service, and support. While sales of stand-alone systems have dominated activities in the personal computer market, the market for units with networking capability for office applications holds tremendous potential. Both new and established computer and office product companies are jockeying for the lead in the race for the "office of the future." Competitors include well-known mainframe computer makers such as IBM and Burroughs, communications companies such as ATT and Northern Telecom, and office equipment suppliers such as Xerox, Wang, and many others. Manufacturers of minicomputers, which are already widely used in distributed data processing applications in offices, are also active in this market. The better-known minicomputer firms include Digital Equipment, Hewlett-Packard, Data General, Prime, Datapoint, and IV-Phase Systems. Microcomputer companies face stiff competition in this market, and marketing requirements appear to pose a major problem.

Networked work stations and higher-priced stand-alone systems are marketed directly to large customers. Manufacturers generally use their own sales forces to call on these accounts. The sale of office systems requires a long selling cycle. Significant field design, installation, and service requirements are involved. However, single orders can be large, particularly from network users. The functions required in a office system network are also somewhat different from those needed in stand-alone systems. The primary functions of office systems include word processing, electronic mail, spreadsheet analysis, filing, bookkeeping, graphics, and budgeting. The ability to integrate several of these applications with each other is considered to be a major competitive advantage. In some systems, for example, a manager can write a report using word processing software, include a table of numbers produced by a spreadsheet analysis, and use a spreadsheet calculation to produce a graph to be included in a report. Several new software packages with this capability, including VisiOn from Visicorp and 1-2-3 for the IBM personal computer, were introduced in 1983.

Personal Computers for Home Use.   With over 90 million households in the United States, the home market for personal computers holds great opportunity. As of January 1983, it was estimated that saturation of this segment amounted to less than 4%. On the other hand, the recent success of low-cost ($100 to $500) home computers, especially Sinclair, Atari, and Commodore models, indicates this segment is beginning to show rapid growth.

The technological requirements for a home system are not great. A powerful microprocessor and large memory are not necessary for a home computer. Home computer software requirements are not sophisticated, except to the extent that software must be easy to use and be largely self-teaching. Other factors are critical to success in the home market. Cost is one; a complete price well under $1000 is necessary to generate a high volume of sales. Also, most individuals have never had first-hand experience with computers, and a great deal of fear and mystery (cyberphobia) are still associated with them.

Distribution and promotion of home systems differ significantly from distribution and promotion of office systems. Relatively high volumes and lower selling prices dictate the use of mass distribution channels. Atari and Commodore are both available in department, discount and large drug stores. Sinclair markets its computers largely through mail-order channels. Dealer training and other sales support are necessary to differentiate one computer from another in this market, yet the lower margins and greater number of retail locations make this part of the marketing program very costly.

Competing successfully in the home market appears to require commitment to a large advertising program. Most ad campaigns seek to capture the attention of both adults and children, educate the audience about the advantages of home computers, and differentiate one brand from the competition. The software available for home systems would include games, word processing, filing manager, budgeting, educational packages, and programming languages.

Science and Engineering Market. Applications of microcomputers in science represents a specialized segment that requires high technical abilities. While much smaller than the office market, scientific applications offer potential high margins due to a premium on high performance. Retail prices for these systems range from $5000 to $30,000. Uses include design and manufacture of integrated circuits and other engineered products. These computers can replace the drafting table with computer-aided design (CAD), and can generate the code to control a manufacturing process (CAM, or computer-aided manufacturing). The complexity of the graphics and mathematical computations requires fast microprocessors and large memory. The ability to design specialized, sophisticated software is a competitive advantage in this segment. The relatively small number of potential customers and the complexity of the product have led to an emphasis on direct or OEM sales as channels of distribution. Success might also depend more on the rapid application of advances in chip technology, relative to office or home systems. New products in this market such as Hewlett-Packard's Model 9000 or Appolo's desk-top unit offer state-of-the-art computing features, power, and performance.

Education Market. The market for personal computers in schools is large in unit volume, yet extremely sensitive to price. Before personal computers became available, computers in elementary and high schools consisted of time-sharing facilities for the purpose of teaching programming. While programming continues as a primary educational application, much of the standard educational curriculum can be programmed on personal computers. Algebra, Russian, and typing instruction programs, to name just three, were available on personal computers by the summer of 1982.

The ability to sell to school systems depends on low-cost, uncomplicated hardware, large availability of software, and support and service, either from the dealer or from the manufacturer. While profit margins tend to be low, school systems offer the promise of large unit volumes and high add-on sales from software and accessories. Selling to schools also presents the opportunity for a manufacturer to develop strong brand preference and loyalty among a large consumer segment at an early and impressionable age.

Minicomputers

While microcomputers should be thought of as computers priced below $10,000, minicomputers range in price from $10,000 to over $1,000,000. Minicomputers are generally thought of as machines that are sold on an OEM basis to systems houses or to end users for industrial applications. The systems house or the end user will develop the applications software for the machine and customize the system for a special purpose, such as process control, communications, or scientific use. Systems houses, which installed over half of all minicomputers sold in 1982, often design and develop the minicomputer system in conjunction with the customer. They also install and service the machines.

In the United States and elsewhere, specialized uses continue to account for the majority of minicomputer installations. World sales of minicomputers for all purposes totaled $10.25 billion in 1982.[12] Sales of minicomputers to the science and engineering market accounted for $2 billion of this total. In addition to specialized uses, minicomputers also compete against small general-purpose computers in the small business systems market. Small business systems are computers priced in the minicomputer range but designed to perform fairly standard business accounting, inventory, or information system functions. Would sales of small business systems totaled $6.6 billion in 1982; about one-third of this total can be attributed to traditional minicomputer makers.

Minicomputers can be sold as stand-alone units to provide central computer capacity for a small organization or department. In the case of departmental uses, the minicomputer is often hooked up to a central mainframe to permit exchange of data and processing flexibility. This type of application is called the distributed data processing segment of the minicomputer market. Distributed processing involves connecting a minicomputer to another minicomputer or a large mainframe through hardwire or telecommunications links. This practice permits transfer of data, flexibility in system capacity, preprocessing, and more efficient use of machine time. These benefits are important in the office systems market. Minicomputers are also widely used as data entry systems for larger mainframe computers.

IBM is the largest supplier of distributed minicomputer systems; others with significant activity in this area in order of 1981 placements are Datapoint, Honeywell, Texas Instruments, Hewlett-Packard, and IV Phase Systems. Shipments of minis for distributed processing applications grew at an annual rate of 65% in 1982. Compatibility with IBM mainframe equipment is particularly important in a number of segments in this market.

Table 14   Minicomputer Market Segments (Based on $ Shipments)

Segment	Percentage of World Minicomputer Market in 1980
Traditional mini computers (OEM and science)	60.3
Small business systems	23.3
Data entry systems	9.5
Office systems	4.5

SOURCE. Datamation.

The key growth segments of the minicomputer industry at present, in addition to distributed processing, are 32-bit machines and nonstop systems. A 32-bit minicomputer processes data in units of 32 bits, as compared with the older 8-bit or current 16-bit processing systems. The new generation of 32-bit minicomputers is dominated by DEC with an estimated 56% market share in 1982. Other contenders include Prime (12.5%), Data General (7.4%), Perkin-Elmer (6.3%), and Wang (4.5%). This market is in the initial stage of expansion at present and should show high growth rates in the early 1980s.

The nonstop computer market was initiated by Tandem Computer Company in 1979. Tandem machines offer dual CPUs so that downtime can be eliminated. These units have sold well to users whose operations are sensitive to computer failure. Tandem has a virtual monopoly in this market, but new competitors such as Synapse are emerging.

Small Business Systems

The lines between the minicomputer and mainframe markets have become increasingly blurred. DEC's VAX series of "super-mini's" competes head-on against small mainframe models such as IBM's 4300 series. The 4300 itself is being used in applications formerly reserved for minicomputers. Other mainframe producers have introduced low-capacity general-purpose machines in traditional minicomputer segments. Nowhere is this overlap more apparent than in the small business systems market.

Small business systems range from desk-top microcomputers to small mainframes controlling distributed processing systems. A small business system is defined here as any general-purpose business computer with a base price between $10,000 and $150,000 for a system configuration. Users of these computers generally fall into one of two groups: small companies buying their first computer, or large enterprises that already have a large, general-purpose computer. Small companies might use these systems for inventory control, billing, maintaining mailing lists, or figuring payrolls. Large companies purchase these systems principally as departmental data processing systems.

In the United States, both market segments are growing rapidly, and competition is increasing, particularly as the distinction between small mainframes and minicomputers diminishes. Sales in the United States exceeded 200,000 systems in 1982, with a value of over $3.5 billion.[13] Estimates indicate that the market could reach an annual volume of as much as 900,000 systems in 1985. The largest competitor in this market is IBM, with its systems 34 and 38, 8100, and related lines. Other U.S. mainframe manufacturers such as Burroughs, Honeywell, and NCR also are active in the market. Leading minicomputer makers, such as DEC and Wang now play important roles in this market.

The U.S. market accounts for about half of world minicomputer and small business systems sales, and U.S. companies are the dominant suppliers in world markets.

The Japanese market for minicomputer and small business systems achieved sales of $1.8 billion in 1982. The major market outside the United States is Europe, and European producers are particularly active in this industry.

The European Market. European producers of minicomputer and small general-purpose systems have been highly successful in retaining control of a large share of their domestic markets. One source estimates that indigenous European producers control 65% of this $4.5 billion market.[14] The leading sellers of minicomputers in Great Britain are ICL, Ferranti, GEC Computers, Systime Ltd., and Plessey. ICL, better known as a seller of mainframes, is also active in the minicomputer and small business systems market. Ferranti's computer sales of $175 million are entirely in the areas of production control and military applications. GEC's minicomputer sales totaled $45 million in 1981. Systime Ltd. began in 1972 as a DEC system house. It now produces its own minis, and realized sales of $60 million in 1981. The U.K. government's National Enterprise Board owns 26% of Systime's equity. The remainder of this highly profitable and fast-growing firm is privately held. Plessey's minicomputer line is highly regarded in some circles, although sales have yet to reach a significant level. These five firms control over half of the British minicomputer market.

The German small computer market is also dominated by European suppliers. Nixdorf holds 29.5% of the German small computer market, followed by Kienzle (12.6%), Philips (12.1%), Triumph-Adler (10.2%), Olivetti (8.1%), Ruf (7.4%) and IBM (3.2%). Nixdorf is the third largest contender in the overall European computer market, behind IBM and CII-Honeywell. Another privately held, profitable, and fast-growing company, Nixdorf has expanded its operations in the U.S. market to sales of over $150 million in 1982. Total 1982 sales exceeded $1 billion. The Deutsche

Bank took a 25% stake in the company in 1979. Triumph-Adler, the second leading German producer of small computers, is owned by Volkswagen. This company is expanding from its typewriter base into a range of data processing and office equipment markets. Total sales in 1982 exceeded $800 million. Triumph-Adler acquired Pertec Computer Products, a U.S. producer of small computers, in 1979. Kienzle, with computer sales of $232 million in 1980, ranks in the top European vendors, ahead of such U.S. rivals as Data General. In addition to these German firms, Siemens also entered the small computer market in 1979.

The French small computer market also exhibits strong domestic firms. Thomson holds 21% of the French mini-computer market. The great majority of Thomson Informatique's 1981 sales of $497 million were in the mini-computer market. CII-Honeywell and Compagnie Generale Electricite also are active in the French small and mini-computer markets. Another major producer of small computers is Logabax. Logabax was rescued from bankruptcy in 1981 when the new Socialist government backed a joint rescue effort by St. Gobain and Olivetti. Logabax has affiliates in Britain, West Germany, Italy, Spain, and Belgium. Logabax is also a major producer of printers. The ultimate status of French firms in this market, as in other areas of the information technology sector, awaits the reconfiguration of the firms nationalized by the Mitterand government.

The success of European competitors in the small and medium-sized computer segments is even more important in light of growth patterns in various segments of the European market. Minicomputers, here defined as systems priced between $10,000 and $400,000, will exceed the total dollar volume of the European mainframe segment for the first time in 1983. This segment is expected to grow at a 22% rate in 1983, while mainframes are growing at only an 8% rate in Europe.[15]

The U.S. Mainframe Market

The mainframe market can be broadly defined to include any general-purpose computer selling for more than $400,000. The bulk of the mainframe market, however, is for systems with purchase prices in excess of $1 million. This segment is the largest single market in the computer industry. Worldwide sales of large general-purpose computer systems exceeded $25 billion in 1982. Sales in the U.S. totaled $12 billion; the European market exceeded $8 billion, and sales of mainframes in Japan approached $3 billion.[16]

Customer requirements in the mainframe sector are quite distinct from those in other segments. The actual hardware represents a small fraction of the entire product package. Installation, education of operating personnel, maintenance agreements, service, and software development account for over half of the total cost of these systems. Many suppliers of mainframes respond to this cost structure by focusing primarily on the central processing unit (CPU) of the mainframe system. Plug compatibility is the key to success with such a strategy. The CPU must be able to run existing software and connect to existing peripherals if such an approach is to be successful. Amdahl, the most successful of the firms pursuing this strategy, was formed in 1970 to sell IBM-compatible CPUs. Amdahl sales of plug-compatible computers exceeded $500 million in 1982. Amdahl is of course owned partially by Fujitsu, and its CPUs are built in Japan. The second largest seller of plug-compatible CPUs is National Advanced Systems (NASCO), an affiliate of National Semiconductor which sells machines produced by Hitachi. NASCO's sales in 1982 were almost $250 million. Other suppliers of plug-compatible machines are Two Pi Corp., an affiliate of Philips N.V., Magnuson Computer Systems, and Control Data. These firms each have sales of $25 to $50 million in the market. Total sales of plug-compatible systems approached

$1 billion in 1982, compared to world mainframe systems sales of about $15 billion for IBM.

Other suppliers of mainframes are dominated by a group of companies known as the BUNCH—Burroughs, Univac (Sperry), NCR, Control Data, and Honeywell. Each of these firms sells entire systems with unique software and technologies.

Mainframe Computer Makers' Sales in 1982

IBM	12,000
Honeywell	551
Burroughs	1,255
Sperry	917
NCR	1,027
Control Data	633
Amdahl	335
NASCO	230
CRAY	102

Segments in the mainframe industry are largely defined by user classes. NCR, for example, realizes over one-third of its sales in the banking market. Control Data is active in the science and military applications market. Cray hold 90% of the market for supercomputers—the largest and most powerful machines.

The European Mainframe Market

The mainframe market has long been the focus of government support in Europe. ICL and CII-Honeywell-Bull are creatures of the British and French governments. Neither company has been financially successful, but both have established significant market positions, primarily but not completely in their home countries.

There have been repeated attempts by major European mainframe producers to combat scale inefficiencies and capital requirements through collaborative ventures, such as Unidata, formed in 1976 by CII, Philips, and Siemens. CII's withdrawal to form a joint venture with Honeywell scuttled this agreement. The presently evolving relationship between CII and Olivetti reflects another attempt to increase competitiveness through collaboration. More recently, collaboration agreements with Japanese producers have been common in Europe. Fujitsu sells medium-sized and large mainframes on an OEM basis to Siemens. An agreement was signed with ICL in 1982, which commits ICL to marketing Fujitsu mainframes in exchange for access to semiconductor technology. Hitachi mainframes are sold by Olivetti and BASF.

Mainframes are the core market for Europe's largest computer companies. These companies are expanding their activities in other areas very rapidly, however. Siemens, which already has an internal semiconductor business, has acquired four U.S. producers of semiconductors since 1979. The largest of these companies, Advanced Micro Devices, is a leading firm in the U.S. industry. Siemens is expanding its activities in the medium-sized and small computer segments in Europe and the United States with its 6000 series of office computers. Siemens is also active in the peripherals market.

Another giant of European industry, Philips, is also active primarily in the semiconductor, small business systems and peripherals markets. It has entered the plug-compatible mainframe market through its U.S. affiliate, Two Pi Inc. Olivetti, while relying heavily on Hitachi for its mainframe product line, has expanded aggressively in other segments. It recently acquired Docutel, a leading U.S. producer of automatic bank tellers, and has been a leader in this market in Europe. With sales of $120 million, Olivetti is also the leader in the emerging European word processing market. The company has minority interests in several U.S. semiconductor and equipment makers, and is also active in the U.S. personal computer market. Olivetti is somewhat unique in that 80% of its sales are generated outside of its home market.

ICL has also been successful in developing foreign markets for its products. Approximately half of its sales were realized outside the United Kingdom in 1982. The 1977 acquisition of Singer's installed base contributed to its presence in the U.S. market. In addition to its agreement with Fujitsu, ICL owns 20% of Computer Peripherals Inc., a joint venture with Control Data (60%) and NCR (20%).

CII-Honeywell-Bull's future is intimately tied to the strategy of the Mitterand government. The socialist government has nationalized literally every major French participant in the information technology sector. It is certain that restructuring will take place, possibly with a larger role for CII. An integrated producer of components, computers, and communications equipment will emerge in France, and CII may provide the nucleus for its formation.

PERIPHERALS

Computer systems of all sizes require a variety of peripheral devices. The most basic of these devices are printers, data storage equipment, and terminals. Although most leading computer makers manufacture at least some of their own peripherals, there are many specialized, independent producers of printers, terminals, data storage and other peripheral equipment. The peripherals segment in both the United States and Japan consists primarily of such firms.

Printers

Worldwide printer sales in 1982 totaled about $6 billion, with the United States accounting for just over half of the total market. Captive production by computer system makers accounted for $2.7 billion of the total; the remainder was generated by independent producers. However, well over half of the sales of independents were to computer systems companies on an OEM basis. Leading nonintegrated producers in the United States are Teletype, Dataproducts, Centronics, Qume, Tally, Diablo, and Printronix. These seven firms accounted for almost half of total printer sales by independent firms in the United States in 1982. Several of these firms are subsidiaries of larger corporations. Diablo, which marketed the first daisy-wheel printer, was acquired by Xerox in 1972. Qume is an ITT affiliate. Tally is owned by Mannesmann of West Germany.

Printers can be segmented into impact and nonimpact models. Impact printers, which accounted for 85% of printer sales revenue in 1982, include traditional typeface or ball characters, dot matrix, and daisy-wheel technologies. Dot matrix printers form letters by series of ink dots. Daisy-wheel printers use a revolving type wheel. While dot matrix printers are much cheaper and faster than traditional or daisy-wheel machines, print quality is much lower and is not yet considered to be at "letter-quality" levels. Daisy wheel units now dominate the small systems market for letter quality printing. Improvements in dot matrix technology may narrow this quality gap. Centronics, Tally, and Integral Data recently introduced dot matrix printers with quality levels approaching those for daisy-wheel machines. While dot matrix print quality is improving, prices for daisy-wheel units are falling rapidly. Recently, daisy-wheel units priced below $1000 have been introduced by Smith-Corona and several smaller companies.[17] Brother International, the aggressive Japanese typewriter producer, Olivetti, and NEC are also active in the low-priced daisy-wheel segment.

The higher-priced segment for impact printers consists primarily of line printers for larger computer systems. The market for line printers is split into speed and quality segments. Dot matrix machines dominate the market for line printers with high speed and limited quality requirements. Daisy-wheel printers compete most effectively in the low-speed and high-quality segment. The high-quality and very high-speed market is served primarily by nonimpact printers.

Although they dominate the high-speed, high-quality segment of the printer market, nonimpact printers compete in all segments. Sales of nonimpact printers totaled $1.4 billion in 1982. There are three principal types of nonimpact printers: thermal, ink-jet, and laser machines. Thermal printers compete in the low-cost, low-speed, low-quality segment. They are widely used in calculators and inexpensive cash registers. Ink-jet machines capable of printing up to 50,000 lines per minute are available at prices ranging up to $700,000 for high-speed addressing systems. Ink-jet printers are uniquely capable of multico-

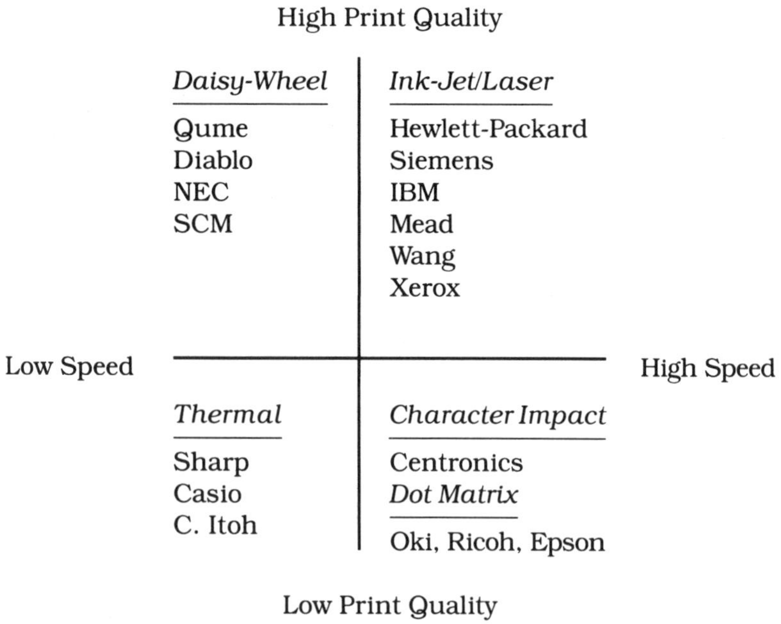

High Print Quality

	Daisy-Wheel	*Ink-Jet/Laser*	
	Qume	Hewlett-Packard	
	Diablo	Siemens	
	NEC	IBM	
	SCM	Mead	
		Wang	
		Xerox	
Low Speed			High Speed
	Thermal	*Character Impact*	
	Sharp	Centronics	
	Casio	*Dot Matrix*	
	C. Itoh	Oki, Ricoh, Epson	

Low Print Quality

Figure 10   Printer segments by technology and competitors.

lor printing and are ideally suited for color graphics uses. Laser printers, although now expensive, offer very high speed, very high quality, and a wide range of applications.

Data Storage Devices

This relatively unheralded segment of the information processing industry rivals the semiconductor sector in size. Worldwide sales of disk, drum, and tape memory devices totaled over $12 billion in 1982. Captive producers account for just over half of all data storage systems sales, but independent producers active in OEM and end user markets are increasingly important in this sector.

The principal product category in the data storage segment is disk memory systems. Data are recorded on oxide-covered disks by electric current passing through the head of the disk drive, creating binary O's and 1's in the oxide. The head then reads data from the disk for use in computer programs. Disk drives can be "hard," with permanent disks, or flexible, with selected disks mounted on the drive and removed on request. Sales of disk drives of all types in 1982 approached $9 billion. IBM, with captive, stand-alone disk drive production valued at about $2.5 billion, is the largest producer. This does not include the value of disk storage incorporated directly in computer systems as original equipment. NCR, Sperry-Univac, Control Data, and Honeywell also have significant captive production, accounting for an additional $2 billion in disk drive output.

Sales of independent producers are split almost evenly between end-users and OEM's. Sales to OEM's totaled $1.8 billion in 1982. The leading OEM supplier is Control Data with 30% of the world market for OEM disk drives. These units are produced by Magnetic Peripherals, Inc., a joint venture with Honeywell. Control Data manages the joint venture and has exclusive responsibility for all sales efforts. Control Data is also active in another main market segment, sales of IBM-compatible units to end users. Its share in the plug-compatible market trails two disk drive specialists, Storage Technology and Memorex.

Memorex, which had been the main OEM supplier of drives to Digital Equipment, was also the leading supplier of IBM-compatible drives until 1978 when it was surpassed by Storage Technology. Memorex held 21% of the IBM-compatible market in 1982, compared to Storage Technology's 43% share. Faced with deteriorating financial performance, Memorex was acquired by Burroughs in 1982 after a merger agreement with Storage Technology collapsed.[18] Storage Technology, with disk drive sales of over $500 million, is the largest independent producer.

An important new segment is the market for microcomputer disk drives. Disk drives for personal computers are produced almost entirely by small independent companies. The market for these drives is exploding, and microcomputer producers cannot meet capacity needs internally. Key producers of low-priced disk drives are Shugart, Seagate, Tandon, and other small entrepreneurial concerns. Shugart, acquired by Xerox in 1980, was the market leader in 1979 with sales of $138 million. Shugart's sales doubled to $270 million by 1982, but the market itself expanded almost tenfold. Tandon, Seagate, and Computer Memories have emerged as major suppliers of disk drives. Shugart spinoffs Quantum and Priam are also key competitors. Tandon has been the leader in the U.S. floppy disk drive market. Tandon shipped over one million disk drives in 1982.[19]

Data Storage Technology

Disk-based data storage equipment uses one of two principal technologies at present. The Winchester and floppy disk drive markets overlap extensively, but do differ in their principal use. Winchester disk drives dominate the higher end of the market. The term "Winchester" comes from the IBM 3030 disk drive, a popular drive with one fixed disk of 30 megabytes and one removable disk of 30 megabytes ("thirty-thirty" is a common term for the Winchester .30 caliber rifle that "won the west"). Floppy disks, utilizing the familiar removable diskettes, are used widely in personal computers. These units usually offer capacity under 400 kilobits, but higher-capacity floppy diskettes are available for larger systems.

At the high end of the mass storage market, new technologies are on the verge of being introduced. Present disk products store about 6500 bits per inch. New thin-film disks made from metal alloys permit storage of 20,000 bits per inch. IBM's 3380 disk drive, introduced in 1983, uses this technology to quadruple disk storage capacity. Its current 3330 disk drive units store 635 million bits; the 3380 will store about 2.5 billion bits. Perhaps even more significant is a new technology based on "vertical storage" of bits. This technology permits storage of over 100,000 bits per inch.[20] Japanese firms including Hitachi, Fujitsu, Sony, and Toshiba are the world leaders in developing this technology, although several small start-up firms such as IBIS, Xidex, and Vertimag (an L.M. Ericsson subsidiary) are pursuing this opportunity. A third emerging technology involves optical storage and reading of data. Matsushita announced a disk drive based on this technology in April 1983. Drexler, a new venture, is another leader in this area.

Terminals

Worldwide sales of terminals reached $9.2 billion in 1982. Terminals have been replacing keyboard/printer data entry and output devices for many years. Cathode ray terminals (CRTs) are now the dominant form of data entry and output. By 1986, an estimated 98% of all data entry devices will utilize a CRT. In the United States, half of all terminals installed are IBM 3270s or compatible products. A base of about 1.5 million 3270-type terminals existed in mid-1983. The 3270-type market is split almost evenly between IBM-produced terminals and compatible products offered by independent producers. Suppliers of 3270-compatible units include a number of smaller firms such as Lee Data, ADDS, Hazeltine, and Lear Siegler.

Other suppliers of mainframes and minicomputers as a whole also produce their own terminals. In the mainframe terminal market, Burroughs, Honeywell, and Sperry together hold an installed base of 400,000 units. In the minicomputer market, DEC has an installed base of 150,000 units; Datapoint and Hewlett-Packard each have about 75,000 units installed, and Wang has almost 50,000 units in place. Major independent suppliers, none of whom hold more than 5% of the market, include Raytheon, Texas Instruments, Zenith, and ITT's Courier Company. Many small independent firms are active in this area in the United States.[21]

The market for terminals is growing rapidly. From an installed base in the United States of about 2.5 million units in 1982, total shipments in 1983 are expected to exceed 800,000 units. The local processing capabilities of these terminals is also growing rapidly. Traditional terminals are considered "dumb" in the sense that they can only be used for information storage and retrieval. New "smart" terminals permit local processing and a wider range of functions. Smart terminals will compete with microcomputers in office automation applications. While shipments of dumb terminals are flat, smart terminal sales are growing at more than 50% per year, and will account for half of all unit sales in 1983.[22] Televideo, a U.S. company founded by a Korean immigrant, is the leading independent supplier of smart terminals. Zenith, Perkin-Elmer, and Ampex are other leading suppliers.

The U.S. market accounts for just over half of world terminal shipments. The Japanese market totaled about $900 million. Sales of terminals in Europe, including captive, totaled $2.2 billion in 1982. European producers, especially Alcatel in France, but also Philips and Plessey, promise to be major contenders in this market. The terminal market is an area with a great deal of overlap between computer and communication applications. Terminals are key elements in videotex and local area network communication systems. Communications equipment producers, notably ATT, are also major producers of terminals.

COMMUNICATIONS EQUIPMENT

The communications equipment industry includes a large number of distinct segments. Many of these, such as radio and television broadcasting equipment, are largely unrelated to the information processing industry. The segments with the most important relationships to data processing are private branch exchange telephone systems (PBXs), data communications equipment, videotex, facsimile, and local network systems. Worldwide sales in these four areas totaled about $12.0 billion in 1982. (Central public switching systems and communications cable sales are not included in this analysis.) The largest of these segments is the private branch exchange market.

Private Branch Exchange

The PBX market worldwide in 1982 totaled approximately $3.5 billion. Sales in Europe were roughly $1.5 billion. In the United States, 1982 PBX sales totaled $914 million. As recently as 1975, ATT held over 80% of the U.S. market. Its share had fallen to 54% by 1981. The leading U.S. producers of PBX equipment are Rolm, GTE, ITT, Stromberg-Carlson, and, of course, ATT. Northern Telecom and Mitel, two Canadian producers, are also active in the U.S. market.

Table 15   The U.S. PBX
Market (1981)

Company	Share
ATT	54%
Rolm	11
Northern Telecom	10
GTE	5
Mitel	4
ITT	3
Others	13

SOURCE: *Business Week.*

Several major new competitors have recently entered this market. Companies such as Wang, Harris, and MA/COM have developed innovative digital PBXs with extended features such as voice and data communication (previous PBXs offered voice transmission alone). Digital PBXs, which transmit data in bits similar to those used in computer systems, are rapidly displacing traditional analogue systems around the world. IBM, which has sold PBXs in Europe for some time, recently won approval from the Federal Communications Commission to offer a PBX system in the United States. IBM also entered an agreement covering a digital PBX system with Rolm in 1983. Honeywell acquired a producer of PBXs in 1981, as did Motorola. Additional entries by computer companies are inevitable.

The European market for PBXs is an area of major activity at the present time. Leading European makers include L.M. Ericsson, Philips, Siemens, AEG, CGE, and Thomson. Other companies are making concerted efforts to enter the European PBX market. Olivetti entered into a licensing agreement with Northern Telecom in 1981 to manufacture small PBXs. In Great Britain, Plessey produces small PBXs under license from Rolm, GEC holds a license from Northern Telecom, and Ferranti is active in a joint venture with GTE.

The role of the national telephone and telegraph authorities (PTTs) is particularly important outside the United States. In Great Britain, for example, all PBXs smaller than 100 lines have had to be purchased from the national British Telecom Board. The small PBX market accounts for 50% of all switching system sales in the United Kingdom. British Telecom serves this market on an OEM basis, purchasing systems from Mitel, Philips, and Plessey. As a result of this arrangement, Plessey has sold more small PBXs than any other producer in the world.

The market for communication equipment is opening up, however. In the United States, communication deregulation is offering increased opportunity to independent vendors. Japan's NTT has opened its procurement doors to foreign suppliers. British Telecom's monopoly on small PBXs was removed in 1982. These steps will increase the level of competition in this industry. ATT is already operating in markets outside of the United States for the first time since it was forced to divest foreign affiliates such as Nippon Electric Company and ITT in the 1920s. The emergence of large global competitors can be expected. In addition, entry by firms from other segments of the information technology sector is inevitable. United Technologies acquired Stromberg-Carlson's communication division in 1982, for example.

Videotex

Videotex is an area where neither American nor Japanese rivals hold competitive leadership. Videotex systems, which are based on home terminals capable of interaction with central data bases, libraries and services, are most highly developed in Western Europe. The most aggressive projects are operating in France, under the sponsorship of the Direction Generale des Telecommunications (DGT). With an annual budget of $5.8 billion, this communications authority has launched several innovative programs. The Teletel project is an experimental videotex system conducted in the Parisian suburb of Velizy. While this experiment involves only 2500 videotex terminals, a larger project consisting of 250,000 user terminals is already well launched. This larger project is essentially an electronic telephone directory and "yellow pages" effort, but plans call for equipping each of France's 30 million telephone subscribers with a free videotex terminal by 1992.[24]

One immediate result of this effort has been the stimulation of videotex terminal production in France. CII-Alcatel, an affiliate of the nationalized Thomson group, was given a contract to produce the first batch of 300,000 terminals in April of 1981. The company has announced plans to produce over a million videotex terminals by 1984.

Other videotex projects of smaller scale are underway in virtually every European country.[25] Prestel, the British effort, currently has about 15,000 subscribers. Plessey supplies terminals for this project. A second British supplier of videotex terminals is Rediffusion, which has installed 120 systems for private customers. In West Germany, experiments in Dusseldorf and Berlin commenced in June 1980 involving 7500 sets.

Japan's videotex system, labeled CAPTAIN, is still in the experimental stage. It is relatively small by European standards. Currently 200 information providers offer services to videotex users, and about 2000 CAPTAIN terminals are in place. In the United States, videotex services are dominated by private companies. ATT's videotex system is in the experimental stages. Two companies, Source and Compuserve, dominate the market at present. These firms sell their services primarily to personal computer owners rather than to individuals or businesses with videotex terminals. Source, with a rapidly growing subscriber list approaching 50,000 users in 1982, hopes to sell 250,000 terminals by 1985. Source recently signed an agreement with Alcatel to sell its products in the American market.[26] Videotex terminals will compete with home computers in the consumer market for information technology products.

Data Communications Products

Two key forces drive the market for data communications products: the networking of computer systems and the expansion of personal computer-based information services. Total sales of data communication products reached $2.6 billion in 1982. The U.S. market accounted for $1.9 billion of this total. The principal segment of this market is accounted for by modems, which convert analogue signals to digital signals for transmission over telephone lines. Sales of modems reached $950 million in 1982. Sales of low-speed modems used by personal computer owners are expected to grow at a 65% rate over the next several years. Other principal products in this market are front-end communications processors, such as packet switches and multiplexers, which accounted for an additional $880 million in sales in 1982. Leading producers of data communications equipment include large established firms such as RCA, GTE, and Motorola but also many smaller and newer companies such as Rolm, RACAL, MA/COM, and General Datacom.

Most data communication passes through modems, multiplexers, or packet-switching processors before being transmitted over telephone lines. PBX products are beginning to appear in this market, but sales of digital PBXs capable of data switching totaled only $60 million in 1982. PBX systems will play an increasing role in data transmission, but telephone-based systems are much slower than transmission via satellite. While normal telephone lines transmit data at 9600 bits per second, satellite systems can transmit data at more than 5 million bits per second. Total revenues from satellite-based data transmission amounted to less than $500 million in 1981, but are expected to be in excess of $1 billion in 1983.[27] Key contenders are COMSAT, Western Union, Southern Pacific Communications, ATT, GTE, RCA, Hughes, and SBS, a joint venture among IBM, Aetna, and COMSAT. COMSAT, a quasipublic corporation, launched the first communications satellite in 1962. It currently operates two satellites for international transmissions and has given over its four units for domestic communication to ATT. The first Japanese communications satellite was launched in February 1983.[28] Western Union, the first firm to launch a private commercial satellite, has five satellites in space. RCA and SBS have each launched four satellites as well. RCA has focused largely on cable TV transmission, while SBS offers a rooftop-to-satellite-to-rooftop system for private transmission of documents, data, and videoconferencing. At present, however, most satellite capacity is being used for telephone and television transmissions, rather than data communications. Despite their current low usage level, satellite systems offer an important vehicle for integrating information processing stations and systems around the world.

A second major new technology, optical fibers, will also speed and influence this process. Optical fibers are being developed that offer transmission speed and quality many times higher than those of conventional coaxial cables. Costs are approaching those for cables and are expected to become competitive in the next year or two. Key contenders in the optical fiber market are Corning, ITT, ATT, and GTE in the United States and Siemens, Philips, GEC, Pirelli, and CGE in Europe. Japanese firms, especially Fujitsu and Hitachi, are also active in this market. The development of fiber-optic transmission media holds an important implication for the entire information technology sector. With fiber-optic transmission media, it is presently necessary to convert electric signals to light and back again for information processing purposes. Work is already well advanced to develop microelectronic circuits that use light instead of electricity as the medium for information processing.[29]

Local Networks

One of the most important trends occurring within the information technology sector is the development of the local network market. The term is misleading because local networks can include not only intrabuilding systems, but also interbuilding, regional, and worldwide communications systems. Intrabuilding systems, such as the Xerox Ethernet or Datapoint ARCNET networks are hard-wired and entail installation of a separate set of coaxial or fiber-optic cables. Linkages for more extended systems include private microwave links and satellite earth station installations. These systems permit the development of worldwide private communication networks for transmission of voice, video, and data signals.

There are many contenders in the local network arena. Datapoint, with over 4000 local networks installed worldwide, held over 50% of the market in 1982. The company suffered severe financial and credibility problems in 1982, however, and larger competitors are now entering this market in earnest. ATT's activities in this area, with its new teleconferencing systems, its AIS network, and enhanced PBX systems such as System 85, are increasingly aggressive. IBM introduced its "token-passing" system for local network architecture in 1982, which will undoubtedly become a major factor in this market. ATT is developing a new standard that will also attract a wide following. Technology standards are presently a stumbling block in this market. There were 43 distinct network systems in the market in 1982, and prospects for definition of a single standard are very limited. The Xerox Ethernet standard has received endorsement from several engineering associations and from major firms such as DEC, Hewlett-Packard, Data General, National Semiconductor, Fujitsu, and Siemens. The IBM and ATT standards will also enjoy considerable support.

Competition at the system standard level is critical, but once standards are adopted, much of the competition in this market will be conducted within distinct niches. The most important niches within this market are for telephone terminals or workstations, data storage devices, satellite earth stations, microwave links, and cable market segments. Small companies such as Microdyne, Scientific Atlanta, and California Microwave are primary competitors in the earth station segment. The microwave area includes firms such as Raytheon and Rockwell.

The local network market will be one of the most dynamic segments of the information processing industry in the years ahead. Contenders from every segment of the industry are vying for a share of this potentially huge market. In some respects this market represents what the larger industry will be in five years, as virtually every piece of nonconsumer information processing equipment sold in 1985 will be integrated in one way or another to some form of internal network. Firms that compete in distinct niches of the information technology sector will need to be very concerned about system compatibility. Firms that attempt to offer their own systems will compete against systems offered by giant rivals.

This review of key industry trends and segments provide the backdrop for analyzing future Japanese activities in the information technology sector. We can now turn to an evaluation of the Japanese positions in these segments today and their strategies for further penetration of world markets.

REFERENCES AND NOTES

1. Captive sales of semiconductors in 1982 totaled about $4.1 billion. The sales of leading producers appear below.

Company	IC Production Value ($ Million)
IBM	2100
Western Electric (ATT)	385
General Electric	225
Delco (GM)	185
Honeywell	180
Hewlett-Packard	160
NCR	70
DEL	60
Burroughs	40
Data General	30
Tektronix	25

SOURCE: *Electronics*, May 19, 1982, p. 135.

2. A. R. Hamilton, "Trends in the Distribution Sector," 1981 Rosen Research Semiconductor Forum, pp. 73–81, *Proceedings of the World Semiconductor Forecast, 1982–84*, Semiconductor Industry Association, Cupetino, California.
3. *Annual Market Survey, Electronics*, January 1983.
4. S. Z. Szirom, "Custom–Semicustom IC Business Report," *VLSI Design*, January/February 1982, p. 38; "The '80's Look in Chips: Custom, not Standard," *Business Week*, January 18, 1982, p. 36.
5. H. Z. Bogert, "The Outlook for Application-Specific IC's," Cupertino: Dataquest, 1983; for a detailed discussion of the custom circuit market, see: *Impact of Custom Circuit Alternatives on Future Product Costs* (San Jose: Strategic Incorporated, 1983).
6. An excellent primer on semiconductor technology can be found in: W. G. Oldham, "The Fabrication of Microelectronic Circuits," *Scientific American*, September 1977, pp.

110–128. See also: T. M. Fredericksen, *Intuitive IC Electronics* (New York: McGraw-Hill, 1982).

7. A fourth technology with relevance solely to the memory sector is bubble memory. Bubble memory sales in the United States in 1981 totaled $70 million; the only other market for this technology was Japan, with sales of $45.5 million. Texas Instruments and several other U.S. producers have withdrawn from this market in the last two years. Texas Instruments had invested up to $100 million in bubble memories before dropping out in 1981. See: *Business Week*, June 22, 1981, pp. 91–94. Rockwell and National Semiconductor also dropped out of the business in 1981.

8. "NEC Will Mass Produce 256 Kilobit RAM chips," *Japan Economic Journal*, October 27, 1981; "Hitachi Will Mass Produce 256k RAM Chips Next Fall," *Japan Economic Journal*, December 22, 1981.

9. The history of the microprocessor is presented in R. N. Noyce and M. E. Hoff, Jr., "A History of Microprocessor Development at Intel," *IEEE Micro*, February 1981, pp. 8–21.

10. Estimated 1981 European semiconductor sales of American-based companies were as follows:

**European Sales,
($ Million, 1981)**

Texas Instruments	395
Motorola	270
National Semiconductor	205
ITT	197
Intel	168
Fairchild	125
Signetics	108
Other	350

11. "Commodore Close-up," *Infoworld*, April 26, 1982, pp. 12–21.

12. Minicomputers are defined here as specialty-purpose computers sold to systems houses and end users and are

priced between $10,000 and $1,000,000. For sales data, see: "Annual Market Survey," *Electronics*, January, 1983.

13. The market for small business systems priced below $80,000 is described in: "Small System Vendors," *Electronic News*, November 16, 1981, p. 10.

14. "Le Marche European des Ordinateurs," *Vision*, September 1980; some insights can also be gleaned from *Datamation's* annual review of the top 25 companies in the European data processing market, "Tracking Europe's Top 25," *Datamation*, November 1981, pp. 36–41.

15. One publication estimates 1983 growth rates for key market segments in Europe, and segment sales as follows:

Segment	Growth Rate, %	Sales, billion
Medium Systems ($50,000–400,000)	20	$4.7
Large Systems ($400,000 plus)	8	4.1
Small Systems (under $50,000)	26	3.1
Terminals	20	1.6
Word Processors	27	.6

SOURCE: *Data Processing*, November 1980, p. 36.

16. Annual Market Survey, *Electronics*, January 1983.

17. *Business Week*, September 13, 1982, p. 114; "A Push From Japan," *Datamation*, November 1981, pp. 80–85.

18. *Wall Street Journal*, November 11, 1981, p. 36.

19. "Picking the Disk Drive Winners," *High Technology*, November/December 1982, pp. 115–116; "Computer Disks," *High Technology*, January 1983, pp. 47–53.

20. "Disk Technology, A Whole New Ballgame," *Computerworld*, November 29, 1982, In Depth section.

21. "I/O: Preparing for Tomorrow Today," *Computerworld Special Report*, November 29, 1982.

22. "The All-American Success Story of K. P. Hwang," *Fortune*, May 18, 1981, pp. 84–88.

23. "The Electronic Office," *Financial Times*, April 13, 1982, p. VII.
24. "France Goes Flat Out for Clever Telephones," *Economist*, March 15, 1980, pp. 83–84.
25. For a review of various videotape projects, see: "Videotex: Write Large or Small," *Economist*, October 31, 1981, pp. 90–01; *Financial Times*, January 1, 1981, pp. IV–VI.
26. An Export Flood of Low-Cost Terminals," *Business Week*, May 11, 1981, p. 46.
27. "Buyers and Sellers in Space," *Economist*, November 21, 1981, pp. 96–98; "SBS's Services Most by this Year," *Business Week*, January 25, 1982, pp. 76–81; "Sky Wars," *Economist* April 21, 1979.
28. *Japan Economic Journal*, February 4, 1983, p. 1.
29. "Optical Computers," *Scientific American*, February 1983, pp. 85–93.

III

The United States and Japan in the Information Age

5

Atari

*The worst form of gener-
alship is to take a walled
city by frontal assault.*

Sun Tzu

ORIGINS OF THE JAPANESE INFORMATION
PROCESSING INDUSTRY

Japan is the only market outside the United States in
which domestic suppliers control more than half of the
market for information processing equipment. Six
companies—Fujitsu, Hitachi, Nippon Electric, Mitsubishi, Toshiba, and Oki—together account for over 80% of
Japanese production of electronic components, computers, and communication equipment. The high degree of
concentration and vertical integration found in the Japanese industry is the conscious result of 25 years of
government policy.

The Japanese government played a critical role in the
early development of the Japanese information processing
industry. The foundation of government support for the
industry rests on legislation passed in 1957 which exempts
the electronics industry from antimonopoly laws and
provides for direct government subsidies.[1] Assistance

157

originates principally from three public agencies: the Ministry of International Trade and Industry (MITI), Nippon Telephone and Telegraph (NTT), and the Ministry of Finance. Public support appears primarily in the form of direct grants for hardware and software development, low-cost loans, protection against imports, and major purchases of informations processing equipment.

Another major form of support was provided in 1961, when the Japan Electronic Computer Company (JECC) was created. This company was formed with capital provided by loans from the Japan Development Bank. This bank is funded by public trust that administers funds generated through postal savings—which account for about 20% of all savings in Japan.[2] The use of these funds is closely controlled by MITI and the Ministry of Finance. With this funding, JECC purchases computers directly from the manufacturers and then sells or leases them to end users. In effect, the agency holds inventory and arranges financing for the manufacturers.

Financial support through preferential access to Japanese capital markets has been another major factor in the development of the Japanese computer industry. A study conducted by Chase Manhattan Bank in 1980 concluded that the leading Japanese electronics companies' net cost of capital was 9.3% in comparison to 17.5% for their American counterparts.[3]

Government support and coordination of research and development have also been important. From 1962 through 1980, MITI organized and funded four major national projects designed to raise Japanese computer technology to Western standards.[4] The goal of the initial program, called Fontac, was to produce an IBM-compatible mainframe. The participants were Fujitsu, Oki, and NEC. MITI provided half of the funding for Fujitsu to design and develop the central processing unit (CPU), for Oki's work on mechanical peripherals and for NEC's work on magnetic peripherals. Fujitsu and NEC both introduced IBM-compatible machines in the early 1960s as a result of the Fontac project.[5]

In the next phase of development, Mitsubishi, Toshiba, and Hitachi joined the Fontac participants in developing a new generation of higher performance machines. As in the Fontac project, each participant focused on one area of computer technology. Toshiba worked on optical character recognition technology. Hitachi, NEC, and Fujitsu developed the CPU. Oki worked on Kanji character processing, and Mitsubishi on image processing. The project resulted in extension of Fujitsu's and NEC's product lines and contributed to the introduction of Hitachi's and Mitsubishi's original lines of computers.

By 1972 MITI had decided that the industry structure was too fragmented to be competitive in world markets. MITI proposed that the six principal domestic computer manufacturers merge their activities into three groups. To ensure cooperation with this proposal, MITI restricted foreign licensing agreements and withheld financial assistance from JECC. As an incentive to the companies, MITI provided $155 million for the development of a new generation of medium-sized and large computers. Fujitsu and Hitachi worked together to develop the M series of computers, while Toshiba and NEC created the ACOS series and Mitsubishi and Oki and COSMOS series. This generation of machines established the Japanese manufacturers for the first time as legitimate competitors in the world data processing industry. These machines and their derivatives represent the bulk of the present installed base of mainframes in Japan.

The fourth major government program was initiated in 1975 to focus on the next generation of computer technology. This project sought to develop the sophisticated semiconductor technology necessary to achieve price and performance parity with world competitors. The $300 million VLSI (Very Large Scale Integration) Project was completed in 1980. It was largely successful in bringing the Japanese industry to parity in this critical area of technology.

The VLSI Project offers an excellent example of how joint research undertakings are conducted in Japan. A private association, the VLSI Technology Research Association, was formed by Fujitsu, Hitachi, Mitsubishi Electronics, NEC, and Toshiba. Each of these firms contributed funds and personnel to the central research facility, located in NEC's Kawasaki R and D laboratory. MITI provided 29.1 billion yen in the form of "conditional" loans, and the companies contributed 33 billion yen. Under this agreement, the participants can freely exploit the project's results and others can license the technology from MITI. Royalties from these licensing agreements are used to repay the MITI loans. Although conditional loans are common, most current projects are supported by direct grants for contract research.

In addition to hardware technology projects, MITI has sponsored extensive software development activities. During the 1970s MITI supported a two-part project to encourage the production of application programs. The project was designed to produce software modules for five types of applications. Forty major software houses were organized into five groups, one to pursue each category of application. The categories included business data processing, management information systems, scientific and engineering uses, operations research, and automatic control software. The success of this program was limited because coordination was lacking among the groups. The groups worked independently and even produced modules in different programming languages. In an effort to convert the modules into a workable system, MITI formed the Joint System Development Corporation (JSDC) in 1976 with a budget of $25 million. JSDC's task was to transform the five modules so that information could be transferred among them.

Another attempt to stimulate the production of software led to the formation of the Information Technology Promotion Agency by MITI in 1979. This agency was designed to promote software development by giving tax breaks to software houses. Any firm selling software can register a program with the agency. For the next five years, 50% of the licensing revenues from that program are exempt from taxation. In addition, all revenues may be placed in a reserve fund to finance more software development. Only 25% of the amount placed in the reserve fund is subject to tax. The Information Technology Promotion Agency also launched a government-funded Software Technology Center in October 1981. This center is developing software for database management, computer-aided design (CAD), and microcomputers.

To stimulate software development further, MITI has encouraged "unbundling" or separate pricing for software—an unusual practice in the computer industry. Traditionally, mainframe users have purchased hardware and software from one source. One price is quoted for both parts of the system. Increasingly, however, independent software vendors have assumed a greater role in supplying software and services to end users in Japan. In addition, the manufacturers themselves are beginning to charge separately for software.

Several current research thrusts focus on long-term technological breakthroughs. During the 1970s, MITI initiated research into pattern information processing systems (PIPS), and spent over $100 million on development of software for this technology. The aim of this project was to permit recognition and processing of Kanji characters, since the many characters that make up Japanese written language make digital conversion very difficult. The PIPS project ended successfully in 1980, with the development of technology that has extensive applications not only in Japan; image-based processing could become a core information processing technology in the future. A new $110 million program to develop office automation equipment using PIPS technology was started in 1980.

Several other long-term research projects have been initiated in recent years. One major cooperative project is the $90 million Optoelectronics project. Participants include Fujitsu, Sumitomo Electronics, Furukawa Electronics, and Fujikura Cable Works. This joint research facility is located within Fujitsu's Kawasaki complex. The project's objectives are to develop fiber-optic technologies, optoelectronic devices and transmission equipment.

Two other major computer system development programs are just beginning. A total of $150 million is budgeted for the development of a new high-speed scientific computer for meteorological and atomic energy research. This program is expected to run until 1988. Second, the much heralded fifth-generation supercomputer program, a $450 million project, is expected to run until 1990. This project encompasses development efforts for the next generation of microelectronic devices, software and computer system architecture.[6]

Although MITI-sponsored efforts like the Fifth Generation Project are critical to the future of the Japanese industry, the role of Nippon Telephone and Telegraph cannot be overlooked. Research on semiconductor technology in the areas of advanced memory chips, Josephson junction circuits, gallium arsenide chips, and other very high-speed circuitry technologies is largely conducted within NTT. Also, unlike its counterpart in the United States, NTT has no production capacity, and buys all of its switching and computer equipment from Japanese producers. Sales to NTT account for over 10% of the electronic data processing sales of the leading Japanese producers.

By Japanese law, NTT was until recently the only organization in Japan that can act as a data processing utility. This service first began in 1968 when NTT started the Demos-E nationwide time-sharing system. Demos-E also provides a software library to users. A second time-sharing service, DRESS, offers sales management and inventory software, as well as software development services. These two services have about 4000 subscribers in Japan. The computers used by these services were developed jointly by NTT, Fujitsu, Hitachi, and NEC.

NTT plays a major role in product development in the industry. It is also the key center for pure research in information processing technology in Japan. NTT's Musashino laboratory is the leading Japanese research center in digital data switching, VLSI circuits, and memory storage devices. Although NTT has recently been required to open bidding for information processing equipment to non-Japanese competitors, and its time-sharing monopoly has been removed, it will continue to play a major role in supporting the Japanese computer industry.

The Japanese government's efforts to encourage technological development in the computer industry have been highly successful. From licensing virtually all of their technology in the late 1950s and early 1960s, Japanese firms have emerged as equals in many areas of computer technology. In some areas, such as image processing, computer-aided manufacturing, and vertical data storage systems, Japanese firms are world leaders. The Japanese government has played a critical role in achieving this position. However, it would be misleading to attribute the success of the industry solely to government support. The strategy and structure of the industry are increasingly beyond the control or direction of any public agency. The partnerships established by MITI in the early 1970s are no longer in existence. Hitachi and Fujitsu have ceased joint research and development and now offer different operating systems for their jointly developed M-series models. Toshiba has withdrawn from the NEC-Toshiba ACOS mainframe venture, and Oki is no longer collaborating with Mitsubishi on the COSMOS series. Affiliates of IBM, Honeywell, and Sperry Univac, among others, remain powerful independent forces in the Japanese computer industry. These firms still account for about 50% of the installed base in the Japanese mainframe market. In addition, a large number of new entrants have appeared in the Japanese computer industry. Firms such as Ricoh, Canon, and Minolta from the office copier industry are aggressively entering the small business systems market, as are calculator and consumer electronics companies such as Sony, Casio, Sharp, and Matsushita. With the exception of the large mainframe area, the domestic industry has become much more fragmented in the last five years.

The market itself has changed dramatically in recent years. In the 1960s and early 1970s, large mainframes accounted for the bulk of Japanese computer sales. Today, although mainframes are still important, other segments of the industry are growing much more rapidly. Industry participants are increasing their emphasis on chips, peripherals, and personal and small business computers. The traditional orientation toward mainframes as the center of the information processing industry, which has long conditioned American and Japanese thinking about the computer industry, is changing rapidly in Japan.

Despite these changes in the market and rising fragmentation in the industry, certain generalizations can be made about Japanese strategies in the information processing industry. A high degree of uniformity exists in the strategies employed by leading companies. This consistency is most clear in Japanese activities in the semiconductor segment.

SEMICONDUCTORS

Each of the six leading Japanese companies in the information technology sector places a heavy emphasis on semiconductor activities. Investments for semiconductor plant and equipment by these firms exceeded $650 million in 1982. NEC, the leading Japanese producer of semicon-

ductors, devoted over 60% of its capital budget to semiconductor facilities in 1982. The other major producers
exhibit a similar emphasis. These six firms presently
account for more than 80% of the Japanese chip market
and 20% of the world market.

While Japanese firms have established semiconductor
production facilities in Europe and the United States, they
rely, as in other industries, primarily on exports to serve
foreign markets. Japanese semiconductor exports exceeded
$1.4 billion in 1982. The United States was by far the
largest export market, with Hong Kong, Taiwan, and
Singapore and South Korea following. Sales to watch
producers and other consumer electronics makers in these
Asian countries account for a large share of Japanese
exports. Sales in the United States cover a wider range of

Table 16   Japanese Semiconductor Exports
            ($ Thousands)

Country	1981	1982 (First Half)
United States	389,182	239,409
Hong Kong	134,247	64,530
Taiwan	141,439	59,888
Singapore	89,586	55,809
West Germany	79,804	53,798
South Korea	130,376	52,040
Brazil	37,770	19,105
Malaysia	29,076	16,159
Philippines	40,333	16,067
United Kingdom	22,726	16,025
Mexico	18,273	7,105
France	19,305	6,691
India	15,539	4,566
Ireland	6,942	4,172
Total	1,237,664	657,503

SOURCE: JETRO.

applications, but the major U.S. markets for Japanese components are in the computer and communications equipment industries.

PERSONAL COMPUTERS

American companies first introduced personal computers in the Japanese market in 1977. In that first year, Tandy, Apple, and Commodore sold 5000 units in Japan. By 1980 there were over 70 firms producing personal computers for the Japanese market. Unit sales exceeded 100,000 in 1980, 320,000 in 1981, and 700,000 units in 1982. Sales of personal computers in the United States, by contrast, exceeded 3,500,000 units in 1982.

Tandy, Apple, and Commodore still represented 80% of the Japanese market in 1979, but the share held by American firms rapidly fell to under 20% of 1982 sales as Japanese companies entered the industry. The major Japanese producers are NEC and Sharp. NEC's PC-8000 alone represents over 40% of the unit sales realized by Japanese companies. Sharp's MZ-80 is the number two model. The top five producers accounted for over 90% of the personal computers sold in Japan by Japanese producers.

Other large Japanese companies have recently entered the microcomputer sector. Seiko, Casio, Sony, and Matsushita introduced models in 1981. Toshiba also introduced its T-100 personal computer in 1981.

Table 17   Japanese Microcomputer Market Shares for 1982 (Not Including Sales of U.S. Affiliates)

NEC	Sharp	Hitachi	Fujitsu	Oki	Sord
43.8%	21.9%	9.4%	6.3%	4.7%	4.1%

SOURCE: *Japan Economic Journal.*

MINICOMPUTERS

In Japan, minicomputers were first designed to meet the internal process control needs of the Japanese computer makers themselves. The range of applications has expanded from that base. Nevertheless, over 40% of the minis in use in Japan in 1981 were used for process control or research purposes. Also, 61% of the minicomputers sold in Japan in 1981 went to systems houses for resale to end users.[7]

The minicomputer market in Japan is small by comparison with other segments of the computer industry. In 1976 the total Japanese market was estimated at only $220 million. The market has been growing rapidly, however. In 1976 about 3000 minicomputers were shipped by Japanese producers. Sales of minicomputers exceeded 16,000 units in 1982, with a value of about $800 million. By contrast, the 1982 U.S. market for minicomputers was estimated at $5.5 billion.[8]

The leading Japanese producer of minis is PanaFacom, Ltd., a joint venture owned by Fujitsu, Fuji Electric Works, and Matsushita. The company supplies minis to its parents and markets them externally. PanaFacom holds about 25% of the Japanese minicomputer market. Hitachi and NEC follow with about 15% of the market each. Digital Equipment K.K., Yokogawa-Hewlett-Packard, and Nippon MiniComputer, a subsidiary of Data General, are the leading U.S. affiliates in the market.

As in the United States, the small business systems market has grown rapidly in Japan. On a unit basis, the growth rate of this segment in Japan has been far greater than the growth rate of the total computer industry. MITI studies show that one-third of the 9482 general-purpose computers operating in Japan in 1970 were classified as small business systems. Two-thirds of the 1979 installed base of 58,944 computers were small business systems. Sales of small business computers in 1982 exceeded 51,000 systems with a value of $1.1 billion.[9]

The leading types of users of small business systems in Japan have remained fairly constant over the years. Wholesalers, retailers, and service businesses make up over 60% of installations. These industries are still made up primarily of small businesses in Japan. Market penetration is yet quite low. Significant growth is anticipated in this sector.

Although the past and potential growth of this segment is impressive, the market is extremely volatile. With many users of limited means, sales of small business systems are more sensitive to general economic conditions than sales of larger systems. For example, in 1975 the oil embargo caused the sales of Japanese general-purpose computers to drop 4.2%. During this same period, sales of small business computers dropped over 35%.

Although over 70 companies produce small business computers for the Japanese market, the top five producers account for over half of the units sold. All of the major computer companies are presently increasing their emphasis on the small end of the general-purpose computer market. It can be argued that, with the exception of Fujitsu and Hitachi, most firms are now placing primary emphasis on small computers. Mitsubishi, NEC, Toshiba, and Fujitsu are the leading competitors in the Japanese SBS market. Mitsubishi's Melcom Series dominates the $5000-to-$45,000 price range, while Fujitsu's V series is the leading $45,000-to-$150,000 system. NEC's Astra series covers the entire price range, while Toshiba's T series is a popular low-priced line.

Other firms also are important in this market. Optic-camera companies and consumer electronics and calculator companies have entered this growing market. Ricoh, Minolta, and Canon are aggressively expanding in this area. Among the calculator companies, Casio and Sharp are upgrading into the market. Consumer electronics companies such as Matsushita and Sony have also introduced small business systems.

Table 18   Companies' Shares of SBS Market in Japan
             for 1982 (Based on Units)

NEC	Mitsubishi	Toshiba	Ricoh	Casio	Fujitsu
14.0%	13.0%	12.0%	8.0%	6.0%	5.5%

SOURCE: Nikkei.

The primary distribution channel for small business computers in Japan has traditionally been independent dealers *(dairiten)*. For example, Fujitsu has a network of 110 dealers throughout Japan. But, as companies such as Ricoh, Casio, and Sharp have entered the market, the distribution pattern has begun to change, with an increased emphasis on retail sales. Toshiba and NEC have developed networks of retail electronics outlets in Japan. Direct distribution networks in Japan are at a similar stage of development as those in the United States.

MAINFRAMES

MITI made the development of mainframe computers a national priority in the late 1960s and early 1970s. The mainframe was the initial focus of the Japanese industry, and it remains the largest segment of the domestic market. Sales of mainframe systems in Japan totaled $2.7 billion in 1982.

Mainframe computer technology was transferred to Japan from the United States in the form of licensing agreements in the 1960s. For example, NEC's long-term licensing agreement with Honeywell only expired at the end of 1982. In addition to licensing agreements, several American computer firms established joint ventures or wholly owned affiliates in Japan. IBM Japan remains the largest supplier of mainframes in the Japanese market. NCR also

Table 19   Mainframe Market
              Share in 1981 (in Yen)

Company	Share
IBM Japan	28.9%
Fujitsu	19.7
Hitachi	15.4
NEC	14.4
Japan Univac	10.5

SOURCE: *Feedback from Fujitsu*, vol. 3,
no. 3, pp. 3, 5.

operates a highly successful wholly owned affiliate in Japan.
Honeywell and Sperry Univac also have significant operations in Japan. Fujitsu, Hitachi, and NEC are the principal domestic players in this market segment. Oki remains
a partner in the Japan Univac KK joint venture.

Japanese companies, although increasingly competitive
in hardware, have been traditionally weak in the software,
service, and support areas of the mainframe market. Many
of these functions are provided by independent support,
software, and systems houses in Japan. These agents
compensate for manufacturers' weaknesses and assist
Japanese computer makers to sell complete systems in
Japan. In foreign markets, weaknesses in these support
areas have been even more pronounced, and external
support services are not as readily available. In response
to this problem, the Japanese computer companies have
tended toward the use of OEM distribution agreements
and plug-compatible product strategies in foreign markets.

SOFTWARE

In their effort to penetrate world markets, one of the major
obstacles for Japanese mainframe makers is software

development. Many observers point out that although the Japanese are competitive in mainframe hardware, they are significantly behind U.S. competitors in software. Since software represents as much as 40% of mainframe systems' costs, and the percentage is rising, this area poses an important challenge for the Japanese computer industry.

Japanese industry has responded to its software short-comings in several ways. Joint software development and distribution agencies formed with government assistance are expanding rapidly in Japan. JECC, the computer leasing agency, serves as a clearinghouse for software programs. Packages filed with JECC increased from 327 in 1978 to 1081 in 1980. Rentals rose from 127 to 8400 over this period. The Joint Systems Development Corporation, a government-backed consortium of 124 software houses employing 16,500 programmers, develops common packages for use by Japanese customers.

Individual companies are also spending heavily in this area. Fujitsu devoted over half of its research and development budget in 1980 and 1981 to software development. It is building a large software development "factory" next to its principal mainframe assembly plant in Numazu at the foot of Mount Fuji. This center employs 1300 software engineers. Other companies have placed similar emphasis on software development.

The number of software engineers employed by the Japanese computer makers appears small relative to the many thousands employed by leading U.S. companies, but this difference can be deceptive because of the Japanese manufacturers' heavy reliance on external software houses. There are about 1800 computer service and software houses in Japan, but the top 50 firms account for about half of the industry's total sales.[10] While nominally independent, these houses are in fact closely tied to individual companies; most of the top 50 firms are directly owned or tied to one of the 6 key computer companies. Fujitsu, for example, works closely with 30 software houses who do most of the company's customer application design and implementation work. Other producers have similar relationships.

The 2 largest software houses, each of which employs more than 4000 people, are owned by Hitachi and NEC. Hitachi and NEC control other houses in addition to these flagship firms. Hitachi formed 11 software subsidiaries between 1978 and 1982—each for a different market segment.

In addition to the traditional software houses, independent systems houses are becoming an important factor in computer marketing in Japan. Such parties have long accounted for the majority of minicomputer sales, but they are now becoming increasingly important in other market segments. These houses tend to be specialized along industry or application lines. Their growth is a key trend in the computer market. Time-sharing companies are also becoming important in Japan. Recently, legislation that had prohibited private companies from entering this field has been repealed. This move has encouraged a number of Japanese firms to enter the field. These time-sharing companies also provide software and other services to users.

All of these efforts are closing the gap in software capabilities. In some areas the gap has already closed. Although Japanese companies are particularly weak in English applications packages, they have strengths in other areas. They are particularly strong in operating systems, manu-

Table 20   Japanese Software Industry Sales ($ Million)

	1976	1977	1978	1979	1980
Software only	$ 287	$ 468	$ 554	$ 794	$ 949
Information services	806	960	1035	1252	1336
Totals:	$1093	$1428	$1589	$2046	$2385

SOURCE: JIPDEC, *General Survey*, no. 48, 1982, p. 15.

facturing control and robotics, advanced utility programs, and database management packages.

PERIPHERALS

Markets for peripheral equipment in Japan totaled about $4.1 billion in 1982. In Japan, the six leading computer makers play a relatively small role in peripherals markets. This condition came about despite the formation of the Peripherals Manufacturers Cartel by MITI in 1969. The cartel, administered by a coordinating committee of the six key firms, standardized designs and allocated production for selected equipment. In spite of the cartel, a large number of entrepreneurial Japanese firms have been successful in entering this market. Companies such as Seiko (Epson), Brother Industries, Toray, Ricoh, Dai Nippon Insatsu, Tokyo Electric, C. Itoh, and Omron are important actors in various segments of the peripherals market.

Japanese activities in the printer market have been most successful in the low-priced dot matrix segment. Japanese firms share in the U.S. low-speed impact printer market rose from 4% in 1979 to 42% in 1982.[11] Oki sold over 400,000 units of its Okidata printers in 1982; over half were exported to the United States on an OEM basis. Epson, a division of Seiko, had even higher unit sales. Its MX-80 model, which sold for under $500 in 1982, was the largest selling dot matrix printer. Its printer is incorporated in the IBM personal computer, among others. Ricoh's dot matrix printer is sold as standard equipment with Radio Shack personal computers. Tokyo Electric recently displaced Centronics as supplier of dot matrix printers to Apple Computer Company. In the daisy-wheel segment, NEC's SPIN-writer is one of the leading low-priced models. SPIN-writer sales in the United States exceeded 50,000 units in 1982. NEC's printers are sold on an OEM basis to Honeywell and NCR, among others.

Japanese firms are increasing their efforts to penetrate the floppy disk drive and Winchester market. Japanese producers dominate their domestic market and are increasingly active in foreign markets. In the United States, Fujitsu markets disk drives through Amdahl, TRW-Fujitsu Corporation, and Memorex. Hitachi disk drives are marketed by National Advanced Systems. Mitsubishi markets its Eagle drives through its U.S. affiliate. Smaller Japanese companies are also active in the United States and elsewhere. TEAC, a world leader in tape memory equipment, is also the main disk drive supplier to DEC. Japanese firms are very active in the disk drive market for personal computers. Alps Electronics supplies the disk units for Apple Computer, for example.

Japanese producers are currently attempting to establish new standards for microcomputer drives and diskettes. Diskettes and drives are now available in 8-inch and 5.25-inch models. The 5.25-inch size dominates the low end of the market. Sony is pushing a 3.5-inch standard while Hitachi has proposed a 2-sided, 3-inch standard for the industry. Verbatim Corporation of Sunnyvale, California, the world's largest supplier of diskettes, and nine other leading producers and OEM customers recently adopted the Sony standard.

COMMUNICATION EQUIPMENT

The Japanese PBX market is less developed than the U.S. and European markets. Private exchanges utilizing digital switching technology have not yet been introduced in the domestic market, although NEC and Fujitsu export such systems. The business telephone market in Japan is dominated by traditional key phone units (phones with push-buttons for different numbers). PBX units, all of the analog technology, accounted for only 658,000 business lines in March 1982, as compared with 4,139,000 single and key phone lines. Only 110 PBX systems were sold in Japan in 1981—20 directly by NTT and 90 by four independent vendors—NEC, Fujitsu, Oki, and Hitachi. NEC and Fujitsu accounted for 90% of sales. These four companies, plus Toshiba, also produced about 65% of all telephone units sold in Japan in 1980, although over 95% of all phone units sales are made through NTT.

While the Japanese market for PBXs is not highly developed, Japanese makers are active in foreign markets. Fujitsu does not offer a digital PBX system in Japan but had sold over 3500 digital PBX systems in the United States by the end of 1982.[12] Those systems are sold under the FOCUS brand name by a wholly owned affiliate, American Telecom, Inc. NEC is the world leader in central digital switching systems for public networks, having surpassed Sweden's L. M. Ericsson in 1981. NEC has installed over five million digital system phone lines around the world. The lack of a well-developed domestic market has not limited overseas activities for these two firms.

One area of communication technology in which Japanese firms are world leaders is the facsimile market. The facsimile market is relatively underdeveloped in the United States and Europe at present. Only in Japan, where conventional telex systems are incapable of transmitting Kanji characters, has this market been actively developed. Sales of "fax" equipment in the United States totaled only $199 million in 1982, as compared with $372 million in Japan. European sales were under $50 million. There were 199,000 fax units in operation in Japan at the end of 1981, and this figure is expected to double by 1984. The introduction of a new "mini-fax" model in 1982 could result in even faster growth. The mini-fax unit—a small, portable, and inexpensive model—attaches to any telephone and uses either the public phone lines or a separate public facsimile communication network to transmit and receive. These units rent for about $15 per month.

Japanese facsimile machine sales and rentals are dominated by private companies. NTT accounts for only 10% of facsimile sales. The leading producer is Matsushita, with about 30% of the market. NEC is second with about 15%, followed by Ricoh (14%), Toshiba (10%), Hitachi (5%), Mitsubishi (4%), Oki (4%), and Fujitsu (4%). A number of U.S. and European producers have recently signed OEM agreements with Japanese facsimile producers. Siemens has linked with Mitsubishi, Burroughs with Fujitsu, 3M with Oki, Exxon with Sharp, and Xerox with Fuji Electric.[13]

The future of the facsimile transmitter segment rests largely on its ability to compete with computerized image and data transmission systems. Electronic mail terminals, networked personal computers, and work stations pose as rivals to facsimile technology. However, Japanese firms appear wedded to the facsimile approach, and they are developing highly sophisticated image processing technology based on the PIPS project. Price and performance trends suggest that facsimile systems will become increasingly efficient. The role of facsimile technology in office systems remains to be seen.

Despite their strengths in these areas, Japanese strategies for the office systems market are not yet highly developed. Japanese offerings in the local network area have not appeared in the market. Office automation projects have tended to focus on word processing applications, an emerging market in Japan, but one that is hindered by the use of Kanji. Efforts to sell word processing equipment in the United States have been abortive. PBX sales represent an area of office system activity for NEC and Fujitsi, but focused thrusts in this market have not yet been defined by other Japanese firms.

FUTURE THRUSTS

As this brief review indicates, Japanese firms are active in every segment of the information processing industry.

Despite this broad base of activity, certain segments will receive priority for future efforts. Which segments are most attractive to Japanese competitors?

In order to answer this question we must consider three basic issues. First, from the Japanese perspective, which segments present the least formidable competition? Likely competitive response has always been a key variable in Japanese sector and segment selection. Japanese firms will prefer to avoid, at least initially, otherwise attractive market segments that are dominated by vigorous rivals. Japanese firms will focus their initial efforts on segments in which competition is least formidable.

This second broad factor to be considered is market attractiveness. Market size and growth rate are important in this respect. Equally important are a set of characteristics that determine the potential applicability of traditional Japanese strategy and strengths. Unit volume, price sensitivity, cost structure, and product standardization are among the variables that measure markets in this dimension. Ability to apply strengths and preferred strategies, while avoiding weaknesses, is the third basic concern in evaluating alternative market segments.

The strengths and weaknesses of the Japanese industry can be defined and assessed in terms of the key success factors for the information processing industry. In order to compete effectively in the industry, firms must possess a number of abilities and resources. Capital requirements in this industry are significant. A technology base and ongoing research skills are very important. Technical human resources are another critical requirement for success in the industry. In addition, sophisticated manufacturing skills are required to produce complex computer systems. Product quality in terms of reliability, ease of use, and price—performance is critical.

Many users in this industry require systems capability from vendors. Successful firms in most industry segments must either have products that are compatible with other system components or be able to deliver a full system to the end user. The system must also be expandable in a number of dimensions; it must be able to add processing capacity and different functions over time.

A direct sales force that can communicate effectively with users about their specific needs can be critical. In some segments, much of the product design is done in the field in discussions between sales personnel and users. A wide range of support functions must also be performed in the field, including education, installation, and maintenance. Service requirements are very important in most segments.

In addition to the hardware requirements in this industry, of course, software is a critical system component. For large, complex systems, vendor credibility is also important. The user must feel comfortable with the vendor in terms of its ability to design, produce, and install a system; to service it, to expand it in the necessary directions, and to provide continuity in the rapidly changing technological environment of the information processing industry.

All of these key success factors are important, but to varying degrees in different segments of the industry. Japanese firms will seek to identify segments in which their weaknesses in terms of these factors are less important, and in which their strengths are critical. The Japanese strengths in these areas fall largely in the first set of success factors. Japanese firms have lower capital costs than their American rivals, and they have an outstanding technical human resource pool. Japanese universities graduated over 20,000 electrical engineers in 1978 compared to 14,000 in the United States.[14] Not only is the pool of graduates larger in Japan, but a significantly larger percentage of Japanese engineers pursue industrial careers. These human resources are the source of growing strengths in the technical area. Although basic research is not yet a competitive strength for Japanese firms, they are extremely effective in commercializing scientific discoveries. Sophisticated and expensive monitoring networks provide an effective substitute for areas of weakness in research and technology. Commercial technology levels are increasingly a strength for Japanese firms. For example, Fujitsu announced its FACOM VP-200 supercomputer in 1982. Although the machine will not be shipped to customers until late 1983, it is presently the world's fastest computer, operating at a rate of 500 million operations per second. In addition to emerging technological strength, traditional skills in the manufacturing area allow Japanese firms to deliver a product of extremely high reliability at a very favorable price–performance ratio.

Although Japanese producers are not viewed as being systems suppliers, each of the major firms possesses the skills and technologies necessary to produce an integrated information processing system. Their current efforts in the market for information processing equipment do not emphasize these system capabilities. In the longer run,

Table 21   Attributes of a Successful Computer
Company and Japanese Strengths
and Weaknesses

Key Success Factors	Japanese Strength/Weakness
Capital	strength
Technology	strength
Technical human resources	strength
Manufacturing capability	strength
Product reliability	strength
Price–performance	strength
Systems capability	weakness
Sales force	weakness
Field support	weakness
Service	weakness
Software	weakness
Vendor credibility	weakness

however, this key factor will become a strength for the Japanese producers.

In several areas however, Japanese firms operate at distinct disadvantages relative to American producers. Outside of their home market, Japanese firms possess little or no direct sales capability. This greatly reduces their presence in a number of key markets. Service and support capabilities are also very weak. Software is another weakness for the Japanese information processing industry. In each of these areas Japanese firms operate at a distinct disadvantage. As a result, they will be inclined either to avoid segments in which these resources and skills are important or to develop strategies for such segments that circumvent, overcome, or limit weaknesses. The most obvious example of such a response is the use of OEM sales and service agreements in the mainframe market.

This analysis of strengths and weaknesses can be useful in evaluating the attractiveness of individual segments of the industry. Figure 11 provides a simple view of the segments in the extended information processing industry. On the vertical axis are a range of product and technology segments, from components and peripherals through very large computers. On the other axis are several broad user segments, including personal computers, business mainframes, office equipment, scientific equipment, and telecommunications equipment. Within this chart a number of relatively distinct segments can be identified. In examining each of these broad segments, we can assess the strength of the principal competition, the characteristics of the market, and the potential for application of Japanese strategies and strengths.

AREAS OF LEAST RESISTANCE

The strengths of existing competitors provide one starting point for assessing the attractiveness of individual

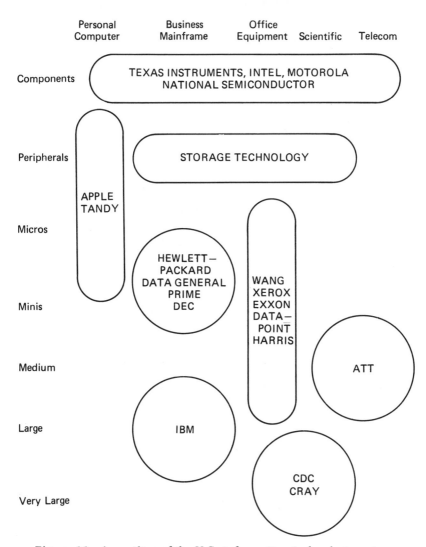

Figure 11 An outline of the U.S. information technology sector.

segments. Japanese analysts would focus on the financial resources of existing suppliers, their share position, the cost and margin structure of their operations, and likely response patterns to new entrants in the market. An assessment of key competitors' definitions of their customer, product, and service focus also provides important input. Analysis of financial and other objectives and policies provides additional insights. Competitors with limited financial resources, with rigid emphasis on profit objectives, with cost structures that do not maximize potential scale economies, and with a limited or incomplete perception of market needs and trends are ideal candidates for displacement. If the industry also exhibits a low level of concentration and a lack of leadership, it will appear even more attractive.

An initial assessment of the segments in Figure 12 suggests several areas that look attractive in terms of the financial resources of major competitors. Key segments of the personal computer and peripheral markets are composed of relatively small competitors with limited financial resources. The component, minicomputer, office equipment, and scientific segments exhibit somewhat larger firms with greater financial resources. The telecommunication and mainframe computer markets contain very large competitors with massive financial resources.

Industry concentration provides another important indicator of attractiveness. Peripherals, components, and scientific instruments also exhibit relatively low levels of concentration. The personal computer segment, while exhibiting a high degree of concentration now, is experiencing increasing fragmentation. High degrees of concentration appear in the minicomputer, mainframe, office equipment, and telecommunications markets. The Herfindahl index used in Table 22 captures not only the traditional concept of market share concentration but also the presence of dominant firms in the market. A Herfin-

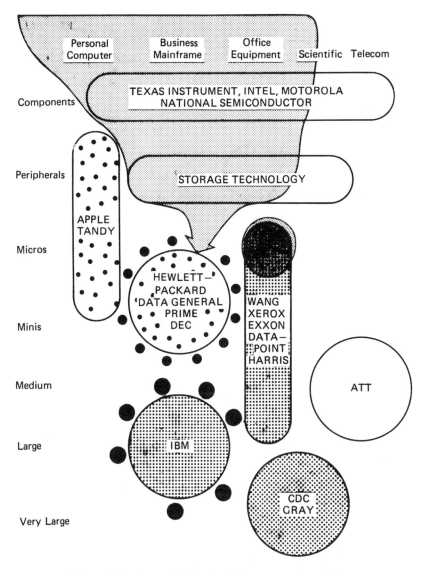

Figure 12 Current thrust of Japanese competitors.

Table 22   Concentration Indices for U.S. Information
Technology Markets (by Dollar Value)

	1975		1980		1982	
	C4[a]	H[b]	C4	H	C4	H
Components	53%	.12	47%	.09	46%	.08
Personal computers	NA[c]		65	.10	51	.09
Peripherals	38	.06	36	.05	33	.04
Minicomputers	71	.22	61	.14	59	.13
Office equipment[d]	84	.31	75	.27	69	.22
Mainframes	78	.29	76	.29	74	.28
Science and military	43	.13	41	.11	42	.11
Telecommunications	87	.48	84	.465	78	.415

[a]C4 measures the percent of total sale achieved by the four largest firms in the market.
[b]The Herfindahl index measures market concentration by squaring and summing the shares of the largest companies in the market.
[c]NA = not applicable.
[d]Includes typewriter, photocopying, word processors, office terminals, and calculating equipment.

dahl index above .25 generally indicates the presence of a dominant firm.

Further analysis is required to assess the cost position, competitive posture, market orientation, and financial policies of key competitors in each segment. Much of this analysis is subjective and potentially deceptive. In several key segments, past trends can be misleading. Competition in the telecommunications industry has been structured by a regulatory environment that no longer exists. Key players in the minicomputer and personal computer industries have been oriented largely toward market development rather than toward aggressive competition. In each of these segments, however, it can be argued that leading firms have striven to achieve cost reduction and market penetration, and that sensitivity to market trends and customer needs has been relatively high. The major exceptions to this observation are repeated failures to perceive market opportunities at the bottom of existing markets. For example, the small copier business in the United States is today a virtual Japanese monopoly. Xerox was late in perceiving and pursuing this opportunity, although a Federal Trade Commission investigation may have delayed entry into this market in the mid-1970s. IBM did not enter the minicomputer market until after it was an established market. Digital Equipment, in turn, is a late entrant into the microcomputer field. Apple Computer has not been a factor in the low end of the microcomputer market. Despite these exceptions, leading U.S. suppliers can be expected to exhibit a high degree of sensitivity to market and competitive developments.

In summary, competitive conditions, as defined by market concentration and the size and financial resources of individual competitors, suggest that peripherals, components, science and military equipment, and personal computers appear most attractive. Telecommunications, mainframes, minicomputers, and office equipment appear least attractive.

MARKET CHARACTERISTICS

In assessing market attractiveness we can examine each of the segments in terms of a number of key criteria that are important to Japanese firms. Japanese strengths and industrial strategy will be most effective in segments where manufacturing efficiency is critical; where product reliability and consistency are essential; and where existing mass distribution channels can be utilized. Japanese strategy will be most effective, in addition, where unit volume is high, price sensitivity is great, product standardization is high, and gross margins are relatively low.

The personal computer market appears to fit these

criteria very well. Unit volume and price sensitivity are high relative to other computer segments; unit margins are not as great as in other markets, suggesting the importance of manufacturing efficiency. Product reliability and consistency are extremely important to both retailers and end users. Pressures for product standardization are high in this segment because of the fixed costs associated with software development. Moreover, the home personal computer segment, in particular, represents an extension of the television market. Japanese video technology, production facilities, brand names, and distribution facilities could be utilized to promote activities in the personal computer market.

The peripherals segment also appears attractive from this perspective. Subsegments such as low-cost printers and disk drives, among others, exhibit high unit volume, high price sensitivity, and high reliability and consistency requirements. Software, sales, and service requirements can be avoided in the OEM market.

The minicomputer market also offers opportunities because of the established role of independent systems houses. However, unit volume is relatively low and gross margins are relatively high compared to those of the peripheral and personal computer segment. The mainframe market exhibits even higher gross margins and more inaccessible distribution channels.

The telecommunications industry offers a variety of subsegments, some of which offer positive characteristics on certain criteria. Telephone sets are sold in very high volume, exhibit a high degree on standardization and some price sensitivity, but lack existing distribution channels. Office key phone, small PBX systems, and telex equipment also exhibit these characteristics but to a less positive degree. Large switching systems are similar to mainframe computers in terms of sales and distribution, customization, and field support requirements.

The science and military systems segment is largely a

closed market, with limited opportunities for penetration. Key subsegments of this market, such as satellite systems, supercomputers, and monitoring equipment, exhibit extremely high levels of customization and low unit volume. Component sales to this segment do offer an important opportunity, however.

The component segment offers perhaps the most attractive opportunity for Japanese industry. Many sectors of the component segment exhibit extremely high unit volume, extreme consistency and reliability requirements, great price sensitivity, extensive standardization, and low gross margins. Manufacturing efficiency in terms of cost and yield is critical in this industry. Distribution requirements are limited because of direct client purchasing arrangements and the existence of compliant independent distributors. The components segment, followed by personal computer, peripherals, and office equipment segments, appears to offer market characteristics most consistent with those favored by Japanese competitors and most likely to allow the successful implementation of traditional Japanese strategy.

A summary of the key criteria for evaluating segment attractiveness appears in Table 23. The numbers in the table correspond to the level of attractiveness to Japanese firms, with high numbers suggesting high attractiveness. Values for different segments are based on our analysis in Chapter 4. They have large margins for error, and there is also no attempt to weigh the importance of different factors. However, analysis of this sort will lead to the identification of several areas that offer an excellent fit for Japanese strategies and strengths.

STRATEGIC FIT

The goal of strategy is to make the most out of what you have. To do this, you need first to have goals which can be

Table 23 A Framework for Establishing Segment Priorities[a]

| | Semiconductor Components | | | Peripherals | | | | | | |
| | | | | Printers | | Data Storage | | Terminals[3] | |
Criteria	Memory	Logic	Micro-processor	Low Speed Low Quality	High Quality High Speed	PC Disk	Mini and Mainframe (OEM + PCM)	Dumb	Smart
Characteristics of:									
Key Competition									
Financial resources	5	5	4	9	6	9	7	7	4
Size	5	5	4	9	5	9	7	8	4
Vertical integration	8	7	6	10	3	9	6	8	4
Width of line	8	7	5	8	5	8	7	8	4
Share of leader	7	8	5	8	5	5	4	8	3
Competitive response record	4	6	4	8	6	5	6	8	3
Cost position	3	5	4	7	7	5	8	9	3
Market									
Concentration	7	7	5	6	6	5	4	10	3
Size	7	7	5	6	4	5	7	6	5
Growth rate	10	9	10	8	4	6	8	7	8
Unit volume	10	4	8	9	4	10	6	8	8
Price sensitivity	10	5	5	8	3	9	5	8	6
Mass channels	1	1	1	3	1	5	2	5	4
Standardization	9	3	5	4	3	3	4	4	3
Customer vendor loyalty	6	3	3	7	4	5	7	7	5

Strategic Fit

Cost structure	10	4	5	8	3	9	8	9	8
Scale economies	10	3	5	8	3	9	6	9	8
Margins	10	3	4	8	3	9	8	9	6
Capital intensity	8	4	5	6	3	8	6	9	8
Manufacturing process	10	4	6	8	5	9	6	9	8
Quality requirements	10	10	10	6	8	10	8	8	9

Strengths/Weaknesses[b]

Capital	8	7	8	7	3	7	6	9	7
Human resources	10	8	9	6	5	6	7	6	7
Manufacturing	10	6	8	9	6	9	7	9	8
Systems	10	9	3	6	4	7	8	5	3
Sales force	10	9	5	5	5	7	8	5	3
Field support	8	7	4	4	4	6	6	5	3
Service	9	8	5	3	1	6	6	9	3
Software	9	8	3	6	3	9	10	9	2
Credibility	9	8	3	7	3	8	8	9	2
Net Assessment (Average)	8.0	6.0	5.2	6.9	4.3	7.2	6.5	7.7	5.1

Table 23 (*Continued*)

	Microcomputers				Minicomputers		Mainframes		Office Equipment	Telecommunications		
Home	SASB[c]	Networked	Portable	OEM	DDP[d]	Small Systems	Large Systems	Word Processing/ Work Stations	LAN[e]	PBX	Satellite Earth Stations
8	6	4	10	5	3	4	1	3	3	3	6
8	6	3	10	5	3	4	1	3	4	4	7
7	6	3	10	5	3	4	1	5	5	4	8
8	6	3	10	4	4	4	1	3	4	5	8
7	7	5	6	4	4	4	2	3	8	3	8
6	7	6	9	5	5	6	1	4	8	6	9
5	6	6	9	6	5	5	3	5	8	6	5
8	7	7	6	6	4	4	2	4	8	6	7
9	7	6	3	5	6	8	8	6	9	7	2
10	10	10	8	5	8	8	5	7	10	8	10
10	6	7	8	5	5	8	2	8	8	6	6
10	6	6	8	6	4	8	2	8	8	7	9
10	7	3	9	NA[f]	2	6	1	7	1	3	5
8	6	4	8	NA	2	6	2	6	1	3	4
6	5	3	8	NA	2	6	2	7	3	5	9

8.2	5.7	4.5	8.4	6.6	4.2	5.8	2.9	6.5	4.6	5.0	7.7	7.7
9	6	4	9	9	6	7	1		5	6	9	9
9	6	4	9	8	6	7	1		4	5	9	9
9	5	4	10	7	5	7	1		4	5	9	9
8	5	5	10	8	7	7	8		4	5	9	9
8	5	3	6	8	4	8	3		2	4	8	8
8	6	4	9	9	6	7	6		4	4	9	9
6	7	8	9	9	9	8	10	8	9	8	8	8
6	7	8	7	9	9	7	10	8	7	6	8	8
9	7	6	8	8	8	9	6	9	4	6	9	10
9	6	3	9	8	2	6	3	9	1	4	9	9
9	4	2	9	8	1	3	1	6	1	3	6	8
8	3	1	9	8	1	3	1	6	1	3	6	7
7	2	1	9	8	1	3	1	6	1	3	8	6
9	3	3	9	8	1	3	1	8	1	9	8	10
9	2	2	9	6	1	4	1	7	3	3	7	9

[a]A factor that is very important to success and that is a Japanese strength would receive a high mark; a factor that is not at all important and a Japanese weakness would also receive a high mark.

[b]Does not include captive producers.

[c]Stand Alone Small Business.

[d]Distributed Data Processing.

[e]Local Area Networks.

[f]NA = Not applicable.

expressed discretely in terms of exports, market penetration, unit cost reduction, or other achievements. The rest entails selecting markets in which you can maximize strengths, minimize weaknesses, and avoid or eliminate competitors to achieve the greatest contribution to these goals. This basic notion drives all strategy. We have already noted that Japanese firms tend to succeed in industries and segments with certain characteristics. Whether such successes are a result of conscious planning or of probing for and pushing through areas of least resistance may be an academic discussion. The point is that certain segments of the information technology sector appear significantly more attractive to Japanese competitors than others. The mainframe market provides a useful example.

Japanese activities in the information processing industry have traditionally been viewed as focusing principally on the mainframe market. Fujitsu and Hitachi, through Amdahl, TRW-Fujitsu, Itel, and NASCO, have been active in the U.S. mainframe market for a decade. It would be very misleading to view this market as the principal Japanese target, however, because this segment is the single segment in which Japanese weaknesses are most important. Sales force, service, support, and software are critical in this segment—more so than in any other. Market conditions in this segment are not conducive to Japanese success. Product standardization is low. Manufacturing costs as a percentage of sales do not exceed 25%, the lowest among all major segments. Price sensitivity is relatively low, and unit volume is also low relative to other segments. Just as importantly, there is a formidable and vigorous competitor in this segment. Although they will continue to be active in this area, Japanese firms are unlikely to launch their principal thrust into world markets in this segment.

Japanese firms have pursued a plug-compatible strategy in the mainframe market and they will continue to do so in the foreseeable future. However, it is virtually impossible to achieve a position of leadership in the mainframe industry by pursuing a plug-compatible strategy. Under such a strategy, someone else dictates the standards and the technology cycles. The Japanese are only followers in this segment; it is unlikely they will be satisfied with such a role. Their activities in this segment can be viewed as learning experience in preparation for a full-scale assault on the market at a later date.

If we focus on the idea that Japanese firms enter markets at the low end, we might expect a major thrust in the personal computer segment. The personal computer segment exhibits a number of very positive characteristics. It has very high unit volume, with high price sensitivity. The potential for product standardization is much higher in this segment than in others. This is a mass market that can be reached through mass distribution outlets. In fact, Japanese activities in the television industry might offer a base for distribution of personal computers. It is a market with tremendous growth potential. At the present time, the key competitors in the business do not appear that formidable. Apple, Tandy, and Commodore, which together account for over 50% of the installed base of personal computers in the world, are relatively small firms with limited financial resources. Although they are vigorous competitors, their ability to survive a protracted price war with well-financed Japanese rivals must be questioned.

If we focus on the second most commonly held preconception of Japanese industrial strategy, we get a second argument in favor of the personal computer market. The long-term perspective of Japanese management, if applied to the personal computer market, could yield powerful results. As noted earlier, most microcomputers priced above $1000 are purchased by small businesses. Over the next 20 years, many of those small businesses will upgrade their computer facilities as their data processing requirements increase. One of the most important characteristics of the information processing industry is the presence of very powerful switching costs. It is very expensive for users to switch from one vendor to another. Such a transition involves expensive modifications of software packages and the development of new infrastructures, retraining of personnel, and new systems architecture. The result is a very high level of vendor loyalty in the industry. One of the ways for the Japanese to overcome this high vendor loyalty is to focus on new users. New users in the computer industry do not enter the mainframe segment on day one. They will emerge from the small business and the minicomputer segments. By focusing on new users in these segments, vendors can ensure themselves of a long-term presence in the mainframe market, as customers upgrade their product and system requirements. As a result, Japanese firms could penetrate the mainframe market without ever competing head to head with existing suppliers.

These factors argue for a strong presence in the personal and small business computer market. Japanese firms are indeed active in these segments, but it is unlikely that the personal computer market will be the main focus of Japanese activity in the near future. The personal computer market is in the very early stages of the product life cycle. Most Japanese firms as yet appear to be relatively uncomfortable in such market environments. The market development requirements in this industry are very extensive. Japanese industry has traditionally been at its strongest when it was able to deliver a standardized product to an educated consumer who was purchasing on the basis of price and quality comparisons. Personal computer customers do not yet fall into this category. They require extensive education and hand holding. Many require direct selling, service and support. Even though software, service, support, and selling requirements are far less rigorous in this market than in other segments, these factors will be an impediment to Japanese penetration of this segment. The development of independent retail, service, and software vendors will reduce this shortcoming, but it will be several years before the effects of such developments will be felt. The existing Japanese base of activity in the television industry cannot be readily accessed by the six leading computer makers, nor can the consumer electronics companies readily access computer technology and expertise.

The segment of principal focus for the Japanese at the present time is of course the semiconductor industry. The semiconductor industry is almost a perfect fit with Japanese strengths and classic Japanese industrial strategy. The semiconductor industry requires no sales force, service, support, or software. The key success factors in this industry are product reliability and price. Key segments in this industry exhibit extremely high unit volume, very high manufacturing content, capital intensity, price sensitivity, and of course product standardization. This segment permits the Japanese to exploit their strengths and avoid their primary weaknesses. The Japanese industrial strategy can be applied effectively in this industry. The market is growing rapidly and competitors are relatively small. Even more important, most of the competitors in this industry are focused almost entirely on semiconductor production. The Japanese firms are highly vertically integrated. They need be less concerned about realizing a profit from semiconductor sales than their nonintegrated American rivals.

Activities in the semiconductor market provide several far-reaching benefits for the Japanese industry. First, by selling components to the external market Japanese firms achieve the economies of scale which permit them to reduce internal sourcing costs to the level of IBM and ATT. Japanese producers use a significant share of their output for internal purposes. Sales of semiconductor devices also provide funding for semiconductor research. Japanese semiconductor research has advanced them to the state of the art in many segments of the semiconductor industry, including VLSI and bubble memories, gate arrays, gallium arsenide semiconductors, and multilayer chips.

Semiconductor technology is critical to success in other

Table 24   Level of Internal
Sales of Japanese
Semiconductor
Companies for 1981

Firm	Percent
Nippon Electric	16.9%
Hitachi	18.5
Toshiba	19.6
Fujitsu	39.1
Mitsubishi	20.0
Oki	28.0

SOURCE: Questionnaire developed by author.

segments of the information processing industry. In the mainframe segment, semiconductor technology is the critical determinant of system performance. By maintaining state-of-the-art semiconductor technology, Japanese producers ensure a speedy response to changes in system standards and technologies introduced by leading American firms. With advanced semiconductor technology, Japanese firms are able to pursue a plug-compatible strategy with relatively low risk of product obsolescence.

But the semiconductor industry is one which exhibits a high level of innovation. How can Japanese firms flourish in such an environment? The answer is that much of the innovation in this industry is process driven. The price-performance characteristics of semiconductor products are a function of bit density. As bit density increases, yields tend to increase reducing unit costs. Bit density is a function of the precision of process technology. That is the only difference between 64k and a 256k RAM.

The semiconductor memory market is the principal thrust for Japanese penetration of the U.S. information processing market. Japanese firms have established a position of leadership in the semiconductor memory market, and they are expanding their activities in the logic and microprocessor segments. This market represents the foundation for Japanese strategy in the information processing industry. While ensuring a low-cost source of semiconductors for Japanese computer and communications equipment, activities in this segment also ensure that Japanese firms will be at or near the state of the art in information processing technology.

An additional benefit of activity in the semiconductor segment is the opportunity to develop supplier connections with firms in other segments of the information processing industry. Japanese semiconductor suppliers are very active in providing components to firms in the U.S. minicomputer, personal computer, office equipment, mainframe, and telecommunications segments. In essence, these activities permit Japanese competitors to establish an initial presence in these markets. While Japanese firms may initially sell discrete components through independent distributors, they can expand their activities into direct component sales and OEM system sales. This line of activity leads Japanese firms ultimately to complete manufacturing of all hardware.

While the hardware would initially be delivered to marketing agents on an OEM basis, Japanese firms could later extend their activities into direct distribution. Japanese suppliers already play an important role in delivering components to their future rivals. If the semiconductor industry is the foundation of Japanese strategy in the information processing industry, it also presents an opportunity for employment of a termite strategy in the existing market structure. Japanese firms can slowly displace rival firms' systems from within through the sale of components. The semiconductor segment is both the foundation for building a new industry structure and a primary vehicle for displacing the old structure from within.

At the same time another segment offers immediate attraction. Certain subsegments of the peripherals market exhibit many of the characteristics most attractive to

Japanese firms. In the low ends of the printer and disk drive markets, high unit volume, product standardization, and price sensitivity are very important. Price and product reliability are essential to customers. In these segments, field sales, support, and software requirements are minimal. Manufacturing efficiency and product quality are key success factors. The sales of peripherals, whether on an OEM or plug-compatible basis, also provide an indirect entree to the market.

Although Japanese activities in the mainframe market have received extensive publicity, the key thrust of the Japanese industry is in semiconductors, and secondly in peripheral equipment. Exports of semiconductors from Japan in 1982 approached $1.5 billion. Peripheral exports exceeded $500 million, while exports of computer equipment totaled only $300 million. The retail value of these computer sales is of course much greater than the export value. These figures are roughly consistent with the current emphasis of Japanese firms in the information processing industry. They also suggest the sequence of focus for Japanese suppliers in this broad market.

Figure 12 (on page 183) describes the present state of Japanese penetration of the U.S. information processing industry. There has already been a widespread thrust into the semiconductor and peripherals markets. These activities permit Japanese firms an initial presence in these segments and an indirect presence in all other segments. The sale of peripherals establishes a Japanese presence around the mini- and mainframe computer installations of their rivals. Sales of central processing units on a plug-compatible basis establish a foothold in the mainframe market.

The next series of thrusts will be threefold. An intial thrust in the small business systems and minicomputer markets can be expected. Over 60% of all minicomputers are sold to systems houses on an OEM basis. That means that the sales, service, support, and software requirements of the customer are met by an intermediary. Despite high switching costs, systems houses will buy minicomputers primarily on the basis of delivery, price, and quality. Japanese suppliers will ultimately find a receptive market in the minicomputer arena. At the same time a related thrust in the small business systems market can be expected. This thrust is closely related to the personal computer market and will seek to establish a potential future customer population in the mainframe segment. The first product introduction planned in the fifth-generation project is the P-SIM microcomputer, a powerful desktop machine for office, business, and professional uses.

A second effort in the mid- to late 1980's will take place in the office equipment area. Japanese copier companies are already beginning to expand into office computer systems. The leading Japanese suppliers are also beginning to produce very sophisticated word processing systems based on pattern information processing technology. These systems will not enter the U.S. market for several years. However, they promise to have a powerful future impact in this segment. Related to these office equipment technologies are the private branch exchange systems offered by NEC and Fujitsu. These products provide the focal point for future Japanese activities in the office automation market. Japanese facsmile processing technology can also be expected to appear in this segment.

A third major thrust for Japanese competitors will appear late in the decade. This thrust will be based on deployment of fifth-generation computer technology. The microelectronic technologies developed in the fifth-generation project will have an immediate impact on the components market. They will also strengthen Japanese offerings in end-product markets. The computer systems that result from this project can be expected to have a very powerful impact on a number of market segments. The fifth-generation microelectronic and software technologies will first be applied in a high-powered microcomputer scheduled for introduction in 1986, but they will support a broad-based thrust across the full range of market segments.

Each of these thrusts will begin to be coordinated by the end of the decade. Japanese suppliers are in a unique position to provide an integrated system to information processing users. The current thrusts of the Japanese industry will begin to merge into a system-oriented strategy. The semiconductor foundation and termite strategy, the encirclement of mainframes by peripherals, and the targeted selection of individual niche markets capable of supporting Japanese activities will give way to a systems orientation. The Japanese suppliers are uniquely positioned to deliver integrated information processing systems. Each of the six leading suppliers possesses the computer, communication, and office equipment technologies needed to compete on a system basis.

This brief analysis provides a projection of Japanese strategies in the information processing industries for the next 5 to 7 years. Japanese activities are already well launched in the semiconductor and peripherals segments. Footholds have already been gained in each of the other segments. The sequence and the speed of events are of course impossible to predict with great accuracy. However, the evolution of Japanese activities in this industry can be predicted with a certain degree of accuracy based on market, competitive, and strategic considerations. This does not mean that Japanese corporations are not opportunistic. Japanese firms respond quickly to evolving market opportunities when they fit with their strengths and weaknesses. In the case of the information processing industry, however, the present conditions and expected paths of market development strongly suggest that Japanese efforts in this industry will follow a particular path and sequence. If we assume that Japanese activities in this industry evolve along the lines presented here, a number of implications for the industry can be developed.

However, the ultimate result of competitive developments in this marketplace depends upon the response of leading U.S. competitors.

The response of major U.S. competitors and of the U.S. government must also be assessed in projecting the likely impact of Japanese activities on the information processing industry. Will the Japanese be able to achieve the same results in the information processing industry that they have achieved in other industries? Results in the semiconductor industry suggest that Japanese dominance of this critical sector is indeed possible. Japanese producers have come from virtually nowhere in 1976 to a strong leadership position in the IC memory market in 1982. The response of U.S. industry and government to this prospect is of critical national importance.

REFERENCES AND NOTES

1. A review of the Japanese government's role in the development of the computer industry can be found in: "The Development of Japanese Computer Industry," E. J. Kaplan, *Japan: The Government Business Relationship* (Washington: Department of Commerce, 1972). See also, "High Technology and Japanese Industrial Policy," A Report to the Subcommittee on Trade, Ways and Means Committee, Congress of the United States (Washington: Government Printing Office, 1980), p. 1–27,

2. The Trust Fund Bureau, which is administered by the Ministry of Finance, reported total deposits of 114.8 trillion yen as of 1982. These funds are derived primarily from postal savings (69.6 trillion yen) but also from deposits into the Welfare Insurance Special Account (27.7 trillion) and annuity accounts. The funds are used primarily in the form of loans, of which a large fraction goes to public agencies like the Japan Development Bank. Trust Fund Bureau loans to the Japan Development Bank account for over 90% of the Bank's total capitalization of 5.4 trillion yen. *Economic Statistics Monthly*, Research and

Statistics Department, Bank of Japan, June 1982, pp. 70 and 76.

3. *U.S. and Japanese Semiconductor Industries: Financial Comparison*, a special report prepared by Chase Financial Policy, a Division of Chase Manhattan Bank (Cupertino: Semiconductor Industry Association, 1980).

4. A description and history fo these related projects appears in "International Competition in Advanced Industrial Sectors: Trade and Development in the Semiconductor Industry," a report prepared for the Joint Economic Committee, Congress of the United States (Washington: Government Printing Office, 1982) pp. 55–102.

5. These machines were the first of Fujitsu's FACOM 230 series and NEC's NEAC line.

6. *Outline of Research and Development Plans for Fifth Generation Computer Systems*, (Tokyo: Institute for New Generation Computer Technology, 1982).

7. "General Survey," JIPDEC Report no. 48, Japan Information Processing Development Center, 1982, p. 8.

8. Annual World Market Survey, *Electronics*, January 13, 1983.

9. *Japan Electronics Almanac 1981* (Tokyo: Dempa Publications 1981), p. 185.

10. "Trends in Japan's Computer Service Industry," JIPDEC Report no. 28, Japan Information Processing Development Center, pp 10–19.

11. "Japan Firms to Expand U.S. Offerings," *Management Information Systems Week*, December 8, 1982, p. 14.

12. Fujitsu Private Branch Exchange Supply Record, Fujitsu Corporation, 1982.

13. "Japan Takes Over in High-Speed Fax," *Business Week*, November 2, 1981, pp. 104–105.

14. These figures are cited by E. F. Kvamme, then Vice President of National Semiconductor Company in Congressional Hearings printed in: "Science and Technology Policy and the Electroncis Industry," Subcommittee on Industrial Growth and Productivity, Committee on the Budget, Congress of the United States (Washington: Government Printing Office, 1981) p. 95.

6

The U.S. Response Today

There were two unique aspects of the move-ment. First, it was not a popular revolution. It was nurtured by a small, dedicated elite. Second, it was instigated by a foreign threat.

M. Y. Yoshino (on the Meiji restoration)

The Japanese initiative in the information technology sector is a powerful one, and it must be taken seriously. Given the national commitment, dedication, and concentration of effort, Japanese activities are guaranteed to have a great impact in this sector. Can they do to this sector what they've done to others? The answer of course depends on the U.S. response. Enough of that response has now been seen so that the question can be answered. No, Japan will not experience the same success in this sector that it has experienced in others. Even though Japan is concentrat-ing its formidable resources in this sector, the response of U.S. industry and government will limit their successes.

The justification for this statement comes from examination of the strength of the U.S. response. The response is indeed powerful, and it will greatly limit Japanese inroads in this market. The information processing industry will not be the first example of a successful American response to Japanese competition. American firms have already proven that they can effectively limit Japanese penetration of world markets. Let me give six examples of industries that almost perfectly fit market criteria that capture Japanese attention. These industries would appear to be extremely attractive to Japanese firms. They are: (1) the low end of the amateur camera market; (2) the consumer power tool market; (3) outboard motors; (4) lawn and garden equipment; (5) chain saws; and (6) tractors. All of these businesses exhibit high unit volume, price sensitivity, high durability and reliability requirements, mass distribution and standardization potential. All require manufacturing skills, capital intensity, and quality control. These markets are perfect for what Japanese firms do best. Japanese firms are active in all these markets, but in no case do these firms hold more than 5% of the world market outside Japan and the Eastern Bloc.

Japanese firms are clearly interested in all of these markets. In each of these industries, there are several Japanese firms trying very hard to expand market penetration. These are not high-priority sectors, perhaps, but they certainly are at least as attractive as others in which Japanese firms have been successful. Yamaha is a major competitor in the piano, organ, and musical instrument market. Honda markets a three-wheel recreational vehicle. Kawasaki sells skimobiles and sea-doos. These industries are certainly no more attractive than the ones we've mentioned. Why do Japanese camera companies sell expensive 35-mm cameras and ignore the larger mass market for amateur photography?

The industries we've mentioned have one thing in common in addition to many of the characteristics that attract Japanese firms. Each of these industries contains a dominant firm that is committed to world leadership in quality, costs, distribution, service, and reputation. Kodak owns over 80% of the market for instamatic-type cameras. Black and Decker dominates the hand power tool business. Outboard Marine Corporation holds over 40% of the world market for outboard motors. The key component in lawn mowers and other gas-powered home and garden equipment is the four-cycle gas engine. Briggs and Stratton holds 55% of the world market for this product. In chain saws, Emerson Electric's Poulan division, which is dedicated to cost leadership in the low end of the market, holds over 30% of unit volume. World agricultural and industrial tractor markets are dominated by John Deere and Caterpillar.

There are some similarities in the way these firms achieved a position of world dominance in their respective markets. First, each adopted early a global perspective on market opportunities and threats. Second, each has been committed to manufacturing efficiency. In the case of Outboard Marine, Briggs and Stratton, and Poulan, this has meant producing virtually all output in a single, specialized location.[1] John Deere and Caterpillar also concentrate over 75% of their output in single facilities. Extensive efforts to standardize product lines can be seen at Black and Decker, Kodak, and Briggs and Stratton in particular. Third, these firms have generally demonstrated a willingness to invest in building market share, distribution channels, and reputations for quality and service. This seems particularly true in the cases of Kodak, Deere, and Caterpillar.

There are other similarities, but the broadest statement we can make about this set of excellent companies is that all of them have adopted and executed many of the elements of strategy used widely by Japanese firms. Most important, they have executed that strategy before Japanese competitors were able to enter the market. After achieving a position of leadership in the market, these firms have vigorously defended their positions. All have demonstrated a willingness to forego profits in the short run to maintain or strengthen their position in the market. As a result Japanese firms have been largely unsuccessful in these markets, despite major efforts.

One of the most intense of these efforts has of course been in the construction equipment industry. Of all the industries listed above, this is the one in which Japanese firms have been most successful. Komatsu has grown to be the second largest firm in the industry. Yet Caterpillar's market share has actually increased in recent years. Komatsu's main thrust has been in the very high end of the market, with units among the largest and most specialized in the industry. Komatsu has been ineffective in the high-volume segments of the market dominated by Caterpillar, and its share of the world market outside of Japan, the Eastern Bloc and Iran is less than 5%.[2]

These American companies have demonstrated how to confront Japanese competition. By implementing a strategy similar in many aspects to that preferred by Japanese companies, these firms have effectively limited Japanese penetration. The Japanese, unable to crack these markets, have moved on to search for easier prey.

If this is how to beat the Japanese, then a similar approach in the information technology sector is in order. Will it deter Japanese advances? No, it will only make them take a detour in their efforts. This sector is too vital and central to fundamental national priorities. No barrier is sufficient to dispel Japanese interest in this sector. The effectiveness of the barriers will influence the speed and level of penetration in various segments of the broader sector, however.

EARLY RESPONSE AT IBM

Response to Japanese competition has been brewing in the U.S. industry for a long time. Recognition of the problem came early. In 1969, Vincent Learson, then president of IBM, stated that Japanese competition would be the key issue for the company in the 1970s. Fred Bucy, President of Texas Instruments, publicly cited Japanese competition as the key threat to the U.S. semiconductor industry in 1975. Active responses were initiated in the 1970s.

IBM was the initial target of Japanese activities in U.S. information technology markets. It has been aware of the Japanese threat for the longest period. IBM is also the first major U.S. firm to respond to Japanese competition.

Japanese activities in the American information processing market initiated in the mainframe computer segment. Fujitsu acquired a 30% interest in Amdahl Corporation in 1971. The founder of this company, Eugene Amdahl, was a former senior design scientist for IBM Corporation. Amdahl formed his own company in order to compete on a plug-compatible basis with IBM central processing units. Fujitsu's acquisition of an interest in the Amdahl operation was intended primarily as a means of acquiring access to Amdahl/IBM technology. Fujitsu's relationship with Amdahl has grown over the last 10 years. Out of an initial relationship which emphasized transfer of technology from Amdahl to Fujitsu, a reverse sourcing pattern has emerged. Fujitsu initially supplied components and subassemblies to Amdahl. Today, Amdahl's central processing units are manufactured almost completely in Fujitsu's Numazu assembly plant. Another leading Japanese computer manufacturer, Hitachi, has followed a somewhat similar strategy in the United States. It also initially emphasized the sale of plug-compatible machines. Hitachi formed a distribution agreement with Itel in the early 1970s. Itel grew very rapidly based on its strategy of leasing IBM-compatible machines. These two agents constituted the principal thrust of Japanese computer makers in the U.S. market during the early and mid-1970s.

IBM's response to these inroads began in the mid-1970s.[3]

Perhaps its most significant strategic move occurred in 1979, when the medium-scale 4300 computer line was introduced. This machine was viewed by many stock analysts with concern. Prices for 4300 models were initially set far below those expected by analysts.[4] The 4300 was priced in such a way that it cannibalized existing lease installations, allowing customers to replace their current machines with ones which generated a much lower rental fee for the same performance. Many analysts concluded that the 4300 did not give a positive contribution to IBM profits. It was a self-inflicted profit reduction. Even though prices were gradually raised over time, the stock market response to this strategy was clear. IBM's stock declined from over $80 per share six months prior to introduction to under $60 six months after (see Figure 13).

The history of the IBM 4300 illustrates a number of critical dimensions of the U.S. response to Japanese competition. It may have been viewed as a financial mistake by some analysts, but it was a strategic success. The 4300 introduction communicated many things to many people. It demonstrated to IBM's customers that the company

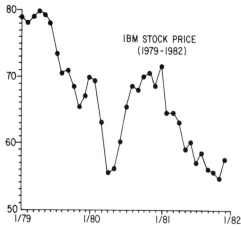

Figure 13   IBM stock price (1979–1982).

continued to be responsive to their needs for improved price and performance. It informed Japanese and other participants in the mainframe segment that there was no "mush" in that marketplace, especially at the low end. The most dramatic impact of the 4300 introduction was of course felt by Itel. Itel revenues from leasing IBM-compatible mainframes had grown from $79 million in 1974 to $564 million in 1977. These machines were supplied primarily by Hitachi. In the wake of a wave of lease cancellations, Itel filed for bankruptcy in 1980.

The 4300 introduction also sent two broader signals. First, it signaled that IBM was willing to forego short-term profits in order to improve its long-term strategic position. This was entirely visible in the pricing strategy for the product. The initial price was extremely low by existing price-performance standards. The radical price break is the key to the second signal. Pricing strategies for the 4300 could have been interpreted as predatory. The second signal is that this issue was not raised by government authorities.

IBM's recent activities suggest that the company is going through a massive shift in strategy and direction. The company's current stated business objectives are to be the low cost producer in the industry; to produce the highest quality product in the industry; and to provide the best customer service in the industry. A number of major steps have been taken to achieve these objectives. In the period from 1979 through 1982, over $6 billion was invested in manufacturing facilities. These new facilities utilize highly advanced process technology, much of it proprietary, and are more automated and capital intensive then any others in the industry. IBM already exhibits one of the most rationalized production systems in the world. Most if its products and components sold in the Western Hemisphere are manufactured at only one site.

A major quality improvement plan has been initiated, with directors of quality control at each facility reporting to a newly appointed corporate quality director. Quality improvement programs, as well as process innovation efforts, are greatly assisted by strengthened labor relations efforts.

New initiatives in marketing strategy have also been launched. Product standardization efforts are underway to improve manufacturing efficiency and product quality. Improved product quality is expected to reduce service requirements. The reunification of the sales force is almost complete as a result of the 1981 reorganization and ongoing field consolidation of divisional sales forces. The result will be that a single face if presented to the customer. The efficiency of the sales organization is expected to increase as a result.

Perhaps even more importantly, IBM has entered mass distribution channels for the first time in its history. Its personal computer is widely sold through independent retailers and the company's own product centers. Efforts to increase sales through noncaptive distribution channels have led to OEM agreements with value-added distributors for the first time in the company's history.

IBM's financial policies have also changed dramatically in recent years. The company had no debt on its balance sheet in 1979 when it placed a $1 billion bond issue, the largest ever issued to that date. An additional $300 million was raised in the sale of bonds to the Saudi Arabian government in 1981. Astute use of American and Saudi capital markets allowed this debt to be taken at a very low cost. An issue of convertible bonds totaling $500 million was announced in 1982, to be issued at an appropriate time. In addition to these new manufacturing, marketing, and financial policies. IBM has continued to invest heavily in research and development. Total spending in this area totaled $1.5 billion in 1982. Basic research and product development work continues unabated but increased emphasis is being placed on value engineering and process innovation.

As a result of these new directions and the company's established reputation and global presence, IBM promises to be an even more formidable competitor in information technology markets in the 1980s and beyond. IBM's ability to use sourcing sties in a variety of countries, its ability to spread overhead and development costs across a range of markets, and its ability to sell a highly standardized product on a global basis will all contribute to cost reduction. All in all, these policies conform quite closely to some of the approaches we discussed in Chapter 1. They represent a new strategic era for the industry.

IBM's preemptive response to Japanese competition will deflect the main thrust of Japanese activities from the mainframe market to other segments of the industry. We already know which segments are most attractive. How will competitors in those industries respond?

SEMICONDUCTOR INDUSTRY RESPONSE

The semiconductor industry has received the primary thrusts of the major Japanese companies. Responses of industry leaders to date have followed several major directions. Of all the leading semiconductor manufacturers, Texas Instruments was perhaps the first to perceive and respond to the Japanese threat in the semiconductor industry. Texas Instruments has been very concerned about Japanese competition in this industry since the mid 1970s. One of Texas Instruments' principal responses to the threat of Japanese competition was the establishment of a Japanese facility for the production of semiconductor devices. Texas Instruments was the first and as of the end of 1980 the only U.S. producer of semiconductors in Japan. Texas Instruments Japan, a wholly owned affiliate, had sales of approximately $150 million in 1982. The affiliate operates three plants. The Hiji plant produces bipolar ICs, the

Hatogaya plant manufactures metal oxide semiconductor (MOS) logic products, and the Miho plant produces MOS memory products, including 64k RAMs. Texas Instruments employs 1800 people in these facilities.

Texas Instruments' second thrust in the mid 1970s was one that is now very common among other producers of semiconductor components. The company attempted to integrate forward into various consumer and computer market segments. Its initial efforts involved entry into the calculator and watch businesses. Although the results of these efforts were largely disappointing, Texas Instruments has established itself as a leader in the home computer market.[5] Sales of home computers, almost entirely through mass consumer retail channels, exceeded 500,000 units in 1982. The company's ability to realize a profit in this business is in question, but it has a strong market position.

The company's strategy in the semiconductor business itself is also being revitalized. Texas Instruments had established itself as the leading competitor in this industry by following a strategy that was not dissimilar from that we have seen employed by successful Japanese competitors. Texas Instruments is a vigorous user of forward pricing. It emphasizes volume production of high-quality, reliable products. One distinguishing feature of TI's strategy is its emphasis on innovation. Texas Instruments has attempted both to be a leader in innovation and to be the high volume producer. Its track record proves its success with this approach. Can Texas Instruments continue to be a low cost producer in the semiconductor industry? An early start in the race for cost leadership, based on technological leadership and the ability to rapidly descend learning curves, could be used to limit Japanese inroads.

We have seen Japanese firms in other industries become more competitive in terms of commercial technology over time. That same phenomenon has occurred in the semiconductor industry. We have noted that Fujitsu was the first to introduce the 64k RAM to the marketplace. Fujitsu was also the first to bring gallium arsenide components to the market. Of course, the underlying nature of innovation in many segments of the semiconductor industry is more closely tied to process than to product technology. New generations of memory products do not reflect a product innovation—they reflect an improvement in process technology. Japanese firms are extremely adept at process innovation. Consequently, any strategy based on the assumption of a technological lead is vulnerable on this basis.

Texas Instruments within the last several years has withdrawn from a number of its existing businesses. The last several years have been very difficult ones for the company. It has been forced to lay off several thousand workers, to liquidate businesses, and to reorganize its vaunted internal management system.[6] It has withdrawn from the low end of the calculator market, and it has withdrawn from the watch business and other consumer product areas. It has also terminated its activities in the bubble memory and selected semiconductor component markets. The company is now returning with renewed vigor to its core markets. At the present time it is emphasizing a renewed thrust into the 64k RAM memory market. Texas Instruments has aggressively expanded its capacity in this area, and it is likely that it will recapture a significant share of this market in 1983.

Other industry leaders in the semiconductor business have followed different response patterns. Motorola, which had already experienced the full brunt of Japanese competition in the color television business, was in the best position to project accurately the impact of Japanese activities in the semiconductor industry. Motorola's strategy has largely been driven by the objective of meeting the Japanese challenge in this sector. A number of steps have been taken to pursue this objective. Motorola has developed some of the most sophisticated labor relations systems in U.S. industry, for example. It has also emphasized product quality and reliability. It is among the leaders in the American industry in improving manufacturing management, customer service, and quality control. Motorola has been less inclined to migrate downstream into consumer product areas which use semiconductor devices. It has, however, increasingly emphasized the more sophisticated segments of the semiconductor industry, such as the microprocessor segment, an area where Japanese firms have yet to establish themselves as legitimate competitors. Motorola has also emphasized the customer relations aspect critical to the development of new applications and uses for semiconductor devices. By emphasizing its marketing and field support capabilities, Motorola has differentiated itself from Japanese producers that are focused on large-volume commodity sales of standardized integrated circuits.

Motorola has also been active in Japan. It was the first American company to win a contract from NTT under the new open procurement system, although the total value of the contract was less than $20 million. It also owns 50% of a joint-venture semiconductor plant in Fukushima Prefecture, and plans to open a wholly owned Japanese plant in 1983. Motorola's broader strategy in the information technology sector is a bold one. It has acquired IV-Phase Systems, a leading supplier of distributed data processing systems, and Codex, a telecommunications company. Its commitment to a strategy based on the sale of fully integrated information systems puts Motorola in select company in this sector.

Intel, widely recognized as the technology leader in the semiconductor industry, has been relatively uninterested in expanding its activities outside of the component business. Its growing emphasis on "silicon systems" has led Intel to become increasingly close to micro- and minicomputer users, and the company is expanding its marketing activities of OEM boards for these machines, but it remains a pure play in the semiconductor business. Such focus and concentration are admirable and consistent with a leadership position, but the risks of this approach are great. Japanese competitors require lower returns on investment in general; in the semiconductor industry the return requirements will be minimal. Japanese firms are vertically integrated and can take profits at other levels of activity; in addition, they realize higher profits in Japan. The profits of the U.S. semiconductor producers are in great jeopardy.

Several important steps have been taken to reduce this exposure. First, Intel has focused its activity in the microprocessor and VLSI logic segments, where it is the leader. Second, Intel is also expanding in Japan. Its sales in Japan exceeded $55 million in 1980. A design center was established in Tsukuba, the new planned national technocenter, and a production facility will be opened in 1983. Third and most important is the agreement with IBM to provide $250 million in funding in exchange for a minority ownership position.

National Semiconductor, regarded as one of the best volume manufacturers in the United States, has followed several of the approaches seen by other leading companies. It launched major, unsuccessful efforts to integrate forward into consumer markets such as watches. It has also established a design center in Japan, but has not yet initiated an effort to commence manufacturing there. National Semiconductor's recent activities appear to focus on working with Japanese companies to migrate into the computer market. National Advanced Systems (NASCO), a wholly-owned affiliate, was formed in 1977 to produce and sell mainframe computers. NASCO ceased production of its own computers in 1983 and now relies solely on machines supplied by Hitachi.[7] National Semiconductor has traditionally been viewed as an excellent manufacturing company with limited innovation skills. Since its strategy closely resembles that of Japanese firms entering this business, it might be asked whether this company is in a position to outcompete the Japanese at what they do best. This is a challenge for any company. The embracing of Japanese firms as potential collaborators would be a common response in such a situation.

Other firms in the industry have largely followed one or more of the broad thrusts seen here. Many have started operations in Japan. Signetics established a Japanese design center in 1981 and plans to open a plant. Advanced Micro Devices will open a Japanese IC plant in 1984. Fairchild will open a Japanese IC plant in 1985. Mostek also plans to build a plant in Japan. Notably each of these firms is owned by a large, well-financed parent company. Many semiconductor companies have been acquired by larger, integrated firms.

The Custom Chip Market

Another emerging response to Japanese competition is the growing custom and semicustom IC market. Custom chips can offer substantial cost savings over standard components for certain applications. Standard components, when used to perform customer-specific functions, are very wasteful of space and circuitry. For example, Network Systems, Inc., a leading producer of communication linkage products for distributed data processing systems, recently replaced a pair of circuit boards with a custom chip. The two boards occupied several square feet, contained over 200 individual components, and cost about $300. The custom chip performed the same function more efficiently, occupied less than a square inch, and cost Network Systems less than $100.[8] Use of a custom chip offers advantages in transmission speed and reliability and, because of space savings, can open up new applications for many products.

Custom chips require extensive interaction with customers in the design phase. Manufacturing efficiency is less critical than for standard components. Users are more concerned about design assistance, delivery reliability, and design security. Unit volume for these products tends to be relatively low, and customer price sensitivity is not critical. All in all, custom chips pose a potentially powerful response to Japanese activities in the semiconductor market.

Cooperative Research Agreements

An additional response with broad implications is the increasing use of cooperative research agreements. Such agreements are rapidly becoming very important in the semiconductor industry. There are many examples. IBM and Texas Instruments are working together to develop the VLSI circuitry needed to connect hardware devices to IBM's new token-passing local area network system.[9] Signetics and Intel have worked together since 1977 in developing microcontrollers for managing interfaces in local area networks. IBM and Motorola have a joint project to shrink the IBM 370 mainframe computer onto Motorola's 68000 microprocessor.[10] Wang Laboratories has cooperative agreements with American Microsystems, a leading producer of semicustom chips, and National Semiconductor. The most ambitious coooperative research effort, the Microelectronics and Computer Technology Corporation, involves eleven major U.S. firms. Many other cooperative design, development, and production agreements exist, and many more will be formed in the near future.

OTHER INDUSTRY SEGMENTS

IBM's response to Japanese activities in the mainframe industry has been vigorous. Other leading firms have also radically changed the direction of their activities. The most extreme example is, of course, ATT.

ATT's transformation from a regulated domestic utility to a global supplier of hardware, systems, and services has only begun, but its implications are far-reaching. ATT's venture into markets outside the United States is not new; the company had extensive foreign operation in the beginning of the twentieth century. ATT shed those international operations in the 1920s; they were assumed by ITT, except in Japan, where they were incorporated in Nippon Electric Company (NEC). Now, ATT is again pursuing world markets for telecommunications systems. ATT International was formed in 1979.

ATT will be selling a wide range of hardware, software, systems, and services in the United States and abroad. The company is active in almost all segments of the information technology sector, with the notable exception of the mainframe computer area. ATT has outstanding semiconductor technology. It introduced a 256k RAM product in 1982, as well as the Bellmac 32-A, a sophisticated 32-bit microprocessor. These are state-of-the-art products in the memory and microprocessor segments. ATT possesses excellent internal minicomputer technology as well, using them as controllers for communications switching systems. The software language UNIX, developed at Bell Labs, is one of the most popular languages for new mini- and microcomputers. The company is also a leading producer of smart terminals. In short, ATT has many strengths outside of its traditional telecommunication business.

ATT's future thrusts in these nontraditional markets are beginning to take shape. The primary current thrust is centered in the company's Advanced Information System (AIS). This system permits users to exchange data among all types of computers and peripherals. Customers can also store data and execute data processing programs on the AIS host computers. AIS is also seen as a base for expanding into data library services, electronic mail, and home information services. The service is primarily seen as applicable first to those smaller companies who do not have internal information processing capabilities. Perhaps more important, it offers a base for future development of a public information exchange network.

ATT initiated work on its AIS program in 1977. Legal questions remain to be resolved, but his service will begin to have an impact on the market in 1983. Other new products will also be highly visible. ATT's Advanced Mobile Phone Service has been in field-test for three years and will be announced in 1983. This service is aimed at the automobile telephone market. The company introduced its video-conferencing system in 1982, a system that permits audio and video reception and transmission from station to station worldwide.

Future thrusts will emerge from ATT's office PBX systems base. In the office systems area, ATT's PBX systems are being upgraded substantially. The minicomputers controlling these systems are being expanded, so that the PBX system can be made to resemble a distributed data processing system when telephone units are augmented by a terminal. ATT is moving toward a direct competition with other suppliers of local area networks and office systems. ATT's System 85 is a PBX-based office system that replaces telephones with terminals.

Internally, the company has undergone a radical reorganization. American Bell, Inc., part of the core split off from the 22 regional phone companies, will control all manufacturing and marketing operations. This company is being organized along lines of business to facilitate entry into a number of new markets. A sales force of 8000 people is being built to sell the forthcoming new generation of ATT products to office and communications equipment customers.[11]

ATT's main markets are presently not experiencing significant Japanese activity. NEC and Fujitsu are increasingly active in the PBX market, but they are by no means

ATT's primary rivals in that marketplace. ATT's primary involvement with Japanese firms has been as a purchaser of communications components. Concern about future competition with these firms has not reached the same intensity within ATT as within other firms in the industry. However, as ATT expands its activities ouside of its traditional and domestic markets, and Japanese firms expand their activities in these markets, confrontations become inevitable. As ATT's strategy evolves toward that of an integrated information system supplier, it will increasingly view Japanese firms as primary rivals. Growing Japanese activities in the PBX, facsimile, fiber-optics, and office equipment markets will stimulate that perspective.

Another firm pursuing a strategy directed toward an information systems approach has a more intimate knowledge of Japanese competition. Xerox has a long history of competition with Japanese rivals. The office copier segment offers a classic example of Japanese industrial strategy. Japanese producers identified and created a new segment of the market at the low end. They dominated this segment through the classic low-price-and-high-quality approach seen elsewhere. Xerox, initially restrained from competing in this segment by a Federal Trade Commission injunction, has recently begun to compete vigorously in the small copier segment. Xerox is rapidly expanding its activities into other segments of the information processing industry. It is active in the word processing business, it has one of the first local networks in the Ethernet system, it offers the Star personal computer and work station, and it is expanding its activities rapidly in the peripherals segment. Xerox owns Diablo, a leading printer supplier, and Shugart, the disk drive maker, among other activities in this area. Xerox is also committed to a strategy based on the sale of integrated information systems. It too will find itself in the race for leadership in this critical market.

Other U.S. companies have followed the same path to varying extents. Vertical integration efforts are apparent at Honeywell, NCR, and Burroughs. All three of these companies are active in the integrated office systems market. Honeywell has acquired Synertek, a semiconductor producer, and Action Communication Systems, a communications equipment company. NCR has acquired Applied Digital Data Systems, a major terminal maker. NCR is also spending over $150 million to double its semiconductor manufacturing capacity. Burroughs has recently acquired Memorex and Systems Development Corporation, an office systems software company.

Other leading firms are also gearing up for the office systems market. DEC's extensive installed base of minicomputers provides an entree for the sale of its networked Rainbow, Decmate, and Professional microcomputers. DEC has greatly increased its borrowing and capital spending to speed entry into fast-growing markets for office systems. Capital spending doubled to $400 million in 1981. DEC's entry into the office systems market closely parallels the efforts of another leading minicomputer maker, Hewlett-Packard. HP introduced a line of office systems in 1981.[12] Wang, already the largest supplier of word processing equipment, is also launching a major thrust at the office systems market. These companies are only the front-runners in a large field of competitive entrants. In short, a wide range of aggressive, talented companies are taking aim at this market.

The cream of U.S. industry is actively pursuing existing and emerging information technology markets. This time out, the Japanese will be competing against a far tougher field on a far tougher course. The competition is bigger, quicker, and smarter. The course has many characteristics that are not conducive to the application of traditional Japanese strengths and strategies. Most important, the referees appear to be taking a different approach in handling this contest.

THE PRESENT ROLE OF THE U.S. GOVERNMENT

Although vigorous corporate efforts are clearly being launched in this industry, it is also obvious that the U.S. thrust is more fragmented than the Japanese effort. Each segment in the U.S. industry is relatively distinct from the others. This condition can permit Japanese firms to focus their efforts on individual segments and dominate them in a sequential manner. The first stage of this scenario can be seen in the semiconductor memory area. The lack of a unified response from U.S. industry is a real likelihood.

Several trends limit vulnerability to this approach. First, leading firms are increasing their degree of vertical integration and the scope of their product lines and market activities. The development of vertically integrated, systems-oriented suppliers minimizes the possibility of a sequential dominance pattern. Second, and perhaps more important, government activities have been highly permissive of this trend and supportive of other means of limiting the likelihood of such an outcome.

The first indications of a new era in govermnent policies toward business could be seen in the late 1970s. Today, it can be said that without doubt, key agencies of the U.S. government are actively protecting and promoting the U.S. information technology sector. A dramatic change in government attitudes has taken place. Skepticism and cynicism about the government's ability to support industry are still widespread, but they will not be for long. A new era in business–government relations has already begun.

Many cries for an enlightened public approach to industrial policy have been heard recently.[13] These calls for action focus on the need for the public and private sectors to work together to improve U.S. industrial competitiveness. It is easy to hear these calls, and easy to agree with them. What may have been missed is the fact that an enlightened joint approach is already well developed in the information technology sector. Government agencies and leaders have been aware of the need for joint efforts in this sector for some time. There is a widespread consensus that government and business must work together to ensure an effective entry in the information technology race. Let me cite 10 examples.

The Department of Defense has been very active in supporting the U.S. information technology sector. The DOD provides the funding for the Very High Speed Integrated Circuit (VHSIC) Project. This project, which will develop the next generation of semiconductor technology, involves more than a dozen major firms, including IBM, Honeywell, ATT, and Motorola. Funding for the project totals over $300 million. The DOD budget also calls for purchases of electronic equipment to grow at a compound rate of over 15% for the next five years. Government purchases account for a large percentage of electronics sales for many companies. Texas Instruments' electronics sales to the govermnent exceeded $1 billion in 1982, for example.[14] DOD funding also supports manufacturing automation projects in the industry.

Virtually every agency in the federal government has taken positive steps to support the competitiveness of the U.S. industry. Antitrust officials in the Justice Department were notably silent following introduction of the IBM 4300. The favorable resolution of the IBM and ATT antitrust suits is another indication of change in policy. More recently, the Justice Department has initiated a predatory pricing suit against Japanese semiconductor memory makers. The Federal Trade Commission has also initiated a suit against the Japanese semiconductor makers. Its suit charges them with monopolistic pricing in the memory market.[15] Simultaneously, the FTC ruled quickly and favorably on IBM's acquisition of a minority position in Intel Corporation, and the Justice Department has decided not to challenge formation of joint research ventures.[16]

The Department of Commerce has been the Reagan administration's point man in negotiations with the Japanese government on trade matters. The Commerce Department has been vigorous in its efforts to open Japanese markets to U.S. imports. NTT's agreement to open its multibillion-dollar procurement business to foreign suppliers was a major accomplishment in this effort.

In the United States, Commerce also has responsibility for reviewing trade complaints. Commerce found Mitsui guilty of dumping steel in the U.S. market in 1982.[17] NEC was accused of dumping communications equipment in the United States in January 1982, just eight months after its first sales of microwave amplifiers to U.S. customers.[18] The Commerce Department also negotiated a voluntary agreement limiting Japanese exports of semiconductors in the United States in March of 1982.[19]

Other aspects of government pressure on Japanese imports take more subtle forms. In 1981, ATT opened bidding for a 776-mile fiber-optic cable system to connect Washington and Boston. The low bidder for the system was Fujitsu. ATT first indicated that Fujitsu would receive the contract, and then awarded it to several U.S. producers. Pressure from several members of Congress and government officials was cited as the reason for the reversal. Fujitsu filed a complaint to the Federal Communications Commission, but its suit was rejected.

Other federal agencies have also gotten involved. The FBI's role in the investigation of Hitachi and Mitsubishi's market research activities in the United States is well known. The IRS has also recently involved itself in a related case. The IRS has been investigating whether Japanese automobile companies underpaid U.S. federal income taxes in the 1970s. The Justice Department went to court in February 1983 to enforce an IRS summons for sales and cost information from Toyota Motor Company.[20]

The impression that it is open season on Japanese firms active in the U.S. market deserves some thought. How could such a radical change have taken place so quickly and quietly at a time when the United States is supposedly experiencing a fascination with all things Japanese? One reason is a growing consensus about the importance of the information technology sector. The United States is in a two-front war against specialized rivals. We compete against the Soviet Union in the military arena, and against Japan and others in the industrial arena. Both are specialized rivals. The USSR neglects its industrial activities to focus on military development; Japan neglects its military to concentrate on industrial endeavors. If the United States is to retain leadership in these arenas, it must dominate those sectors that are critical to success in both arenas. If the United States does nothing else, it must do this. Its leaders know it, and they have taken appropriate actions.

The action extends beyond some of the discrete steps taken by individual agencies. Fundamental changes in the U.S. political economy are taking place. These changes are designed to improve the competitiveness of U.S. industry in this and other sectors. At the most obvious level, public policies with respect to issues such as anti-trust litigation and trade policy have changed radically. Equally profound changes have occurred in U.S. capital and labor markets.

SHIFT IN USAGE OF U.S. CAPITAL

Between 1979 and 1982, over $200 billion was transferred from traditional savings sources to money market funds. This massive shift had a major impact on the usage of American capital. Funds that had been placed in savings and loans to fund home mortgages were transferred to money funds that invested in corporate (and government) paper. The residential housing market was the single largest user of capital in the United States between 1949 and

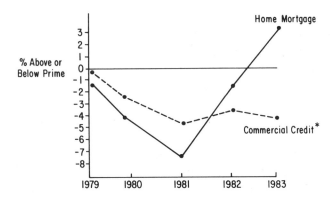

*Prime Commercial Paper Rate/dealer 91-119 days,
Fed. Res.: per Business Week the first week of
January for the years cited.

Figure 14   Housing and corporate finance in the United States.

1979. During most of this period, the average American
could receive a fixed-rate, long-term loan at or near the
prime rate, and the interest on the loan was tax deduct-
ible. The average citizen had better access to capital markets
than the largest corporations. That has obviously changed.
Today, commercial paper markets offer funds to companies at 3 to 4% below the prime rate, while home morta-
gages are well above the prime rate. (See Figure 15). Some
of this difference is due to cyclical trends in money markets,
but much of it appears to be an enduring pattern. This
radical shift has had a devastating effect on the housing
industry and on the average citizen. Yet it is only one of
the prices long paid by Japanese citizens to support their
industrial activities. More will be said on this in the next
chapter.

CHANGES IN U.S. LABOR MARKETS

A similar shift is occurring in labor markets. Union
membership is falling rapidly in the United States. The

AFL-CIO estimates that its membership declined by 800,000 between 1981 and 1983. The membership of United Rubber Workers has fallen from 180,000 to 130,000; membership in the United Steelworkers Union has fallen from 1.4 million to 700,000 since 1981. Union concessions and givebacks have been widespread in recent labor pacts. The wage increase for all union agreements negotiated in 1982 averaged 3.8%, the lowest in over 25 years, while worker productivity increased at the highest rate in over ten years.

A number of new institutional arrangements have helped improve conditions in the labor market. Employee stock ownership plans (ESOP'S) have been widely adopted in recent years. Introduction of an ESOP can be tied to a renegotiation of existing wage and benefit agreements. Share ownership, particularly when accompanied by "new" industrial relations programs, can have a positive impact on worker productivity and commitment. Use of pension fund assets to buy shares in the company can further improve worker commitment.

New labor relations programs, with titles like work enhancement groups, management employee participation teams and more traditional Scanlon plan or quality circle systems, are being widely adopted in American industry. The initial results of these programs are mixed, but there are many success stories. Significant cost reduction and quality improvement benefits can be realized with these approaches.

The shift in labor markets is real. Whether it reflects a temporary shift in bargaining power due to a recessionary environment is another question. Whatever the cause, an enlightened approach to cooperative business–labor relations is essential to an enduring industrial effort. Such an approach is being developed at many companies in the United States today. I for one believe that American unions and management can realize tremendous improvements in industrial efficiency without increasing capital investment. The recent success of a joint union–management program at Jones and Laughlin Steel Company, in a highly unlikely setting, demonstrates some of the possibilities for improvement.[21] Jones and Laughlin has cut its unit labor costs by as much as 60% in some plants, to levels below those of comparable Japanese facilities. It has done so by working closely with the United Steel workers to identify opportunities for redefining job descriptions and factory work structures. In the information technology sector, where unionization is very low, such improvements will be even easier to realize.

SHAPE OF THE FUTURE

These shifts in public policies, capital markets, and labor markets all point in one direction. The United States is committing itself to becoming more competitive in world markets. When these forces are combined with the broad changes that are occurring in managerial philosophy and strategy, the power of the U.S. response can be seen. A unified American response has already been engineered. It is a thrust that will not be readily reversed or altered. I believe it can only intensify. Not everyone would agree with this assessment. This path involves major sacrifices by large segments of American society.

A war cannot be fought without taking casualties. Consumers and organized labor, for the first time in recent U.S. history, are being asked to pay a price to support industrial activities. The prospect of a consumer and labor backlash is very real, and it may be a key concern in the 1984 elections. These groups are being asked to pay a large price to support American industry. If they resist, they could force a return to former policies that favored these groups. There are some signs that such a backlash is occurring. Capital is returning to banks and savings and loans through new money market accounts.

Consumers, especially home buyers, will benefit. The housing industry is also receiving direct assistance in the form of federal housing funds. Trends in labor agreements may reverse once the economy strengthens. A political reversal in 1984 might strengthen these trends and weaken the industrial response.

Even if such a scenario were to develop, it would not have as negative an impact on the information technology sector as on others. Each of the leading Democratic candidates has pledged to support high-technology industries. The so-called "Atari" Democrats have made national support of high-tech industries their principal campaign issue.[22] The election of a Democratic ticket in 1984 would probably only increase direct federal support for the U.S. information technology sector. Domestic political developments in the United States will affect the nature and intensity of public support for the industry, but not its direction. To a great extent, public policies and programs in this arena are irreversible over the next five to ten years.

One other factor will have an equally important role in determining the strength of the U.S. response. That factor is related to the primary reason for past U.S. trade policies with respect to Japan. Political conditions in the Far East are very different today than they were 10 years ago. The primary difference is China. The China card was played against the Soviet Union. It also plays well against Japan. Progress in Sino–U.S. relations will determine the intensity of U.S.–Japanese competition in the industrial arena. The 1983 Shultz mission to China and the forthcoming visit of Chinese Premier Zhao Ziyang are important steps in this regard.

Many things happening in the United States point toward a revival of industrial competitiveness, particularly in high-technology sectors. Changes in public policies, capital markets, labor markets, and management philosophies and strategies have all been stimulated by the success of the Japanese economic system. American academics and managers flock to Japan. The press has strained itself in praise of Japanese industrial accomplishments. Many changes in management philosophies have occurred as a result.

Management philosophies and strategies have undergone a dramatic metamorphosis in recent years. No one can speak for all management, but in many companies, radical changes are taking place in labor relations, manufacturing strategies, inventory management, product engineering, quality control, capital structure, market research, and government relations. These changes offer dramatic and positive proof of a resurgence in U.S. industrial competitiveness.

Other profound changes are occurring in the United States. Personal savings in the United States are rising, partially as a result of concern over the future of the social security system and corporate pension funds.[23] New IRA, Keogh and employee retirement plans provide tax-free vehicles for savings. Within the capital markets, funds are being shifted from traditional savings accounts to money funds, commercial paper markets, and stock and bond markets. This trend will generate more funds to support investments in new facilities and businesses. Research and development partnerships are growing rapidly, and venture capital activity is at an all-time high.

Labor unions have lost much of their power in recent years. The federal government's showdown with the air traffic controllers' union (PATCO) provided an important symbolic victory in the effort to curb union abuses, and to encourage renewed commitment to productivity and efficiency. Union membership is presently declining in the United States.

Public policies are also undergoing dramatic change. Antitrust activity has declined sharply. The two biggest antitrust suits of the past decade, against IBM and ATT, were both resolved positively in 1981. The Justice Department and the Federal Trade Commission have turned their

Union Membership in the United States: Number of Workers Covered by Collective Bargaining Agreements Involving More Than 1,000 Workers (in thousands)

1974	1975	1976	1977	1978	1979	1980	1981	1982	1933
10,200	10,300	10,100	9,800	9,600	9,500	9,300	9,100	9,000	8,500

SOURCE: W. M. Davis: "Collective Bargaining in 1983," *Monthly Labor Review*, January 1983, pp. 3–16.

attention to Japanese companies. All major federal agencies have made positive contributions to the national effort in the information technology sector.

The fact that no central agency has been appointed or established to manage public support for this sector is remarkable in itself. If support for this sector is a central priority, why is there not a Department of Technology or an Industry Department to administer the program? Such concerns could be addressed by the newly-proposed Department of Trade, but support for this effort appears so widespread that a central agency may not be necessary.

There remains the question of coordination. How will the activities of many federal agencies be coordinated to ensure effective support for this sector? That concern raises a more fundamental question. Have the various federal agencies' past activities in this sector been coordinated to date? Extensive high-level policy discussions have occurred in Congressional hearings, in meetings sponsored by groups such as the Council for Military Preparedness, and within the senior councils of the government. Nonetheless, the activities of various agencies appear to stem primarily from a groundswell of opinion within the agencies themselves. Many government leaders reached the same conclusion about the importance of this sector at roughly the same time. A revolution has started in Washington. It is not yet a popular revolution, but one instigated by a small elite. As more people in Washington join in, and, more important now, as more parties in industry, labor, academe, and elsewhere join in, the force of this movement will only get stronger.

If the United States is beginning a virtuous cycle, Japan may be entering a vicious cycle. The sources of Japan's industrial strength are still intact, but many factors are beginning to work against continued expansion. First, free access to foreign markets is decreasing. European markets have never been freely open to Japan, but in recent months entry has become much more difficult for Japanese exporters. As of early 1983, Japanese video cassette recorders must enter France through the "port" of Poitiers, the site of Charles Martel's historic stand against Moorish invaders, where a small but dedicated staff of customs agents diligently examine each unit before it passes inspection. A leading executive in the Japanese television industry described to me a recent round of negotiations with European trade officials:

> We sent three of our best negotiators from MITI. The European Economic Committee was also well represented. I recognized two of their negotiators as employees of Philips [the largest European producer of television].

Similar patterns are occurring elsewhere. Canadian customs officials stalled imports of Japanese automobile imports for over 30 days in the fall of 1982 simply by stricter enforcement of existing regulations. In the United States, the Oakland customs office held up over 13,000 import shipments in late 1981 and early 1982 for as much as six months with a similar effort. Japanese firms have already begun to respond to this growing protectionism by establishing plants overseas. Honda and Nissan operate automobile factories in the United States, for example. Offshore production will limit exposure to trade restrictions, but may result in reduced economies of scale, quality, and productivity. In an effort to address these concerns, Nissan sent the entire work force of its new Tennessee car plant to Japan for training in its home factories at a cost of $70 million. Even if quality and productivity standards can be achieved, however, there is the issue of how offshore production will affect the domestic Japanese economy.

Tougher trade restrictions aren't the only problem facing the Japanese. Their federal deficit in 1982, swollen by growing expenditures, was $70 billion. The deficit may exceed $100 billion in 1983.[24] Public works programs account for the bulk of these deficits, but increased expenditures for welfare programs and defense also contribute to the growing deficits. Public works programs are a cornerstone of the Liberal Democratic Party's 28-year tenure in office. The current administrative reform effort is intent on streamlining losing operations such as the railways, but massive public works continue. U.S. pressure to increase defense spending has been relentless at a time when Soviet activities in the northern islands are a growing public concern. Efforts to reduce the deficit have largely come at the expense of emerging public welfare programs. A program of medical support for the elderly was terminated in the summer of 1982.

The willingness of Japanese citizens to accept the existing order also has to be examined. The next generation may not show the same selfless dedication as their parents, especially since they have not had to face the issue of survival as the previous generation did. Will they pay the same price to further increase their material well-being? Hungry and ambitious Koreans, Chinese, and others are prepared to if they are not. There is nothing to suggest the emergence of a counterculture in Japan, but the willingness of its citizens to continue their unceasing hard work has to be questioned. Such a phenomenon has already been observed in Germany, and it is always tempting to draw parallels between Germany and Japan. Something has happened to the German work ethic in recent years. German workers now receive six weeks' vacation and work 27 hours per week on average.[25] Productivity growth has stopped completely, and the German *wirtshaftswunder* has ground to a halt. The same thing could happen in Japan. Notably, juvenile crime and arrests are increasing dramatically in Japan, and savings rates have declined sharply in recent years.

Meanwhile the United States seems to be undergoing a revival of the work ethic. The mood on college campuses could not be more different than it was 10 years ago. Many of the younger generation in the United States appear intent on making their mark in the business world. This new dedication seems to reflect a return to older values that may be affecting more and more of American society. Religious activity in the United States is increasing rapidly, particularly in fundamentalist groups such as the Southern Baptists. Crime and divorce rates dropped for the first time in recent history in 1982. A grass-roots restoration may well be occurring in the United States. If so, it will combine well with the changes occurring in more elite positions and institutions.

The United States has changed a great deal since 1979, and almost all the changes hold positive implications. This country is going to be a formidable competitor in the years ahead. Japan's position has not improved in recent years. Nonetheless, the Japanese will pursue their goals in the information technology sector with single-minded zeal and determination. It promises to be a very interesting race.

REFERENCES AND NOTES

1. For a discussion of some of these companies' operations, see: "Why Putt-Putt Isn't Sputter-Sputter," *Forbes*, June 7, 1982, pp. 51–52; "The Little Engine That Coins Money," *Forbes*, October 1, 1977, p. 86; "An American Company Honda Can't Mow Down," *Forbes*, July 28, 1980, p. 54.

2. Komatsu, with 1982 sales of $2.6 billion, is the second largest firm in world construction equipment markets. Komatsu's sales represent about 15% of the world market. Its sales of construction equipment in communist markets and Iran, however, totaled more than $500 million, reducing its share of the rest of the world market to less than 5%. See: "Komatsu on the Track of CAT," *Fortune*, April 20, 1981, pp. 164–174; *Japan Economic Journal*, March 15, 1983, p. 1.

3. Ulric Weil, *Information Systems in the 1980's* (Englewood Cliffs: Prentice-Hall, 1983), pp. 339–341.

4. *Bro Uttal* "How the 4300 Fits IBM's New Strategy," *Fortune*, July 30, 1979, pp. 58–63.

5. "When Marketing Failed at Texas Instruments," *Business Week*, June 22, 1981, pp. 91–93; Texas Instruments is cited as the first personal-computer maker to use mass merchandisers in: *Distribution Strategies of Personal Computer Manufacturers*, San Jose, Strategic Incorporated, 1982, pp. vii–62. Texas Instruments holds about 20% of the home computer market.

6. "Texas Instruments in Mid-Life," *Forbes*, March 15, 1982, pp. 64–66.

7. *Computerworld*, February 7, 1983, p. 6; *Wall Street Journal*, February 2, 1983, p. 10.

8. This example was cited in discussion with managers of VLSI Technologies, Inc. For further information on custom semiconductors, see: "Custom–Semicustom IC Business Report," *VLSI Design*, January–February 1982, pp. 32–38; "Superchips Face Design Challenge," *High Technology*, January 1983, pp. 34–42; "The 80's Look in Chips: Custom Not Standard," *Business Week*, January 18, 1982, pp. 36D–36T.

9. "TI, IBM Team on Local Area Net IC's," *Electronics News*, September 20, 1982.

10. "IBM, Motorola Coy Over Mainframe Chip Project," *Computerworld*, November 19, 1982.

11. "American Bell has the Industry Buzzing," *Business Week*, February 7, 1983.

12. "Two Giant Bids for Office Sales," *Business Week*, November 9, 1981, pp. 86–96.

13. See for example; I. C. Magaziner and R. B. Reich, *Minding America's Business* (New York: Harcourt Brace Jovanovich, 1982); D. Heenan, *The Reunited States* (Reading: Addison-Wesley, 1983).

14. *Wall Street Journal*, February 7, 1983

15. "U.S. Probes Japanese Chip Makers" *San Jose Mercury*, July 27, 1982, p. 1

16. "Justice Department will not Challenge Formation of MCC," *Computerworld*, January 17, 1983, p. 79.

17. *Wall Street Journal*, July 19, 1982, p. 4.

18. "Japan's High-tech Sales Hit a U.S. Snag," *Business Week*,

January 25, 1982, p. 40; *Electronic News,* August 10, September 7, 1982.

19. "Japan to Cut Export of Chips to U.S.," *New York Times,* April 8, 1982, p. D1.

20. *Wall Street Journal,* February 7, 1983, p. 4; *Japan Economic Journal,* February 15, 1983, p. 3, states: "It is feared that a similar charge might be made on semiconductors. . . ."

21. "U.S. Steel Snags a Hot Shot," *Business Week,* May 9, 1983, p. 38.

22. For example, Senator John Glenn's high-technology program is described in: *Computerworld,* February 7, 1983, p. 6.

23. U.S. savings rates rose to 8.1% in July 1982. The average rate for the 1971–1981 period was 6.0%. "Why Savings May Stay High," *Business Week,* September 13, 1982.

24. "Fiscal Crisis Will Worsen," *Japan Economic Journal,* February 4, 1983, p. 1.

25. See Klaus Macharzina, "Development and Competitiveness of the German Economy," in M. S. Hochmuth and W. H. Davidson (eds.), *American Challenged: The Changing World Economic Order,* forthcoming 1983.

7

The Amazing Race

Powerful forces are at work in the information technology sector. The Japanese attack has been launched; U.S. industry leaders have begun to respond, and the U.S. government has redefined its role in this industry. The outcome of these three forces will determine the future state of this industry, and much more.

THREE REVEALING MARKET TRENDS

The immediate results can be seen in three market trends. First, the Japanese presence in many market segments has led to a dramatic reduction in prices and profit margins. This trend can be seen most clearly in the semiconductor memory market, where their activities are most advanced. A second source of pressure on prices and profits in other segments is IBM's increasingly aggressive posture. Second, competitive pressures have contributed to an acceleration of technology cycles. New technologies are being introduced more quickly, shortening product life cycles and also reducing returns from research. The semiconductor memory market again provides a good example. The 64k RAM reached commercial volumes in late 1981, but pilot production of 256k RAMs commenced in late 1982. The 512k RAM already is being used in laboratory applications. The combination of declining margins and accelerating technology cycles contributes to the third key trend: a dramatic increase in capital requirements at the very time cash flows are shrinking. Ben Rosen, industry analyst, estimates that the profits of U.S. memory makers as a group declined $400 million in 1982 while capital investment needs rose sharply for those firms committed to this market.

Capital intensity in manufacturing is rising dramatically for semiconductor producers because of the need to automate manufacturing facilities in order to reduce costs. Similar pressures are being felt in other segments.[1] IBM's expenditures on production facilities have totaled over $7.0 billion in the last four years. Digital Equipment's plant expenditures have exceeded $1 billion in the last four years. Massive capital investments will be needed to stay cost competitive in most industry segments.

These pressures are being felt by firms in all segments. With technology cycles quickening, returns shrinking, and development costs rising, many firms are responding by reducing the scope of their activities. For firms active in a range of businesses, a common response has been to reduce or cease activity in marginal lines. The semiconductor industry provides some clear examples of this response. National Semiconductor has terminated its bubble memory line, its consumer product efforts, and its computer manufacturing activities in the last three years. Texas Instruments dropped its bubble memory line, its digital watches business, and a number of semiconductor lines in 1981.

Acquisitions and Joint Development Agreements

Two other main responses can be identified. First, more than 20 U.S. semiconductor producers have been acquired by larger firms in the last three years.[2] The acquiring firms, such as Exxon, Schlumberger, General Electric, United

Technologies, Siemens, and Philips, are large enough to provide the funds needed to remain competitive in the industry. In addition to a wave of acquisitions, the semiconductor industry is experiencing an explosion of joint development agreements. Many firms have engaged in cooperative agreements to reduce the cost and risk of research activity, and to enable themselves to continue to carry a broad line of products. These agreements extend beyond traditional second-sourcing relationships. With the cost of developing a new VLSI chip now approaching $1 million, exchanges of circuit data and masks are becoming more common, and long-term technology pacts are seen more frequently.

Such agreements are not limited to the semiconductor industry. Extensive licensing and cross-licensing activity is occurring in other segments of the industry. The most common form involves one firm's filling its line by acquiring technology or a production source from another firm. IBM signed an agreement with Rolm for PBX technology in 1983.[3] ATT and Philips N.V. entered into an agreement in early 1983 for the joint design and production of tele-

Table 25   Selected Acquisitions of Semiconductor Companies, 1978–1982

Semiconductor Maker	Acquiring Company
Intersil	General Electric
Synertek	Honeywell
American Microsystems	Gould
Signetics	Philips
Advanced Micro Devices[a]	Siemens
Fairchild	Schlumberger
Mostek	United Technologies
Zilog	Exxon
Intel[a]	IBM

[a]Minority investments.

communication equipment.[4] Memorex (Burroughs) and
Control Data have formed two joint ventures to develop
and produce a new generation of IBM-compatible disk
drives.[5] Wang Laboratories has technology and sourcing
agreements for VLSI chips with American Microsystems
and National Semiconductor.[6] Hundreds if not thousands
of such agreements have been signed in the last year. No
firm can be fully self-sufficient in this sector unless it
focuses on a very discrete part of the market.

The Drive Toward Systems

The drive to secure sources of technology and production
results not solely from pressures on capital requirements
for existing businesses. It occurs primarily as a result of
efforts by many firms to become suppliers of information
processing systems, rather than discrete products. A
massive shift toward a systems orientation is occurring
in the industry today. Many firms are trying to expand
their activities so that they can sell integrated systems to
end users. Cooperative agreements provide one means of
expanding the scope of a company's offerings. Other
approaches to building a system capability include internal development and acquisition. The acquisition route
has been widely used by many firms.

Xerox has acquired a number of specialized companies
operating in distinct market segments. Diablo is a leading
producer of printers, Shugart is a leader in disk drives.
Motorola's acquisitions of IV-Phase Systems and Codex
greatly enhance its ability to develop and deliver integrated systems. Honeywell's acquisitions of Synertek,
Action Technology Associates, and other communications
service companies represent an effort to expand the
company's systems capability. Acquisition strategies can
be seen at several other firms. Exxon Enterprises has
acquired a number of firms active in information processing markets, including Zilog and Vydec. MA/COM has

Table 26   Selected Joint Development and Technology Exchange Agreements

Parties	Year	Agreement
Texas Instruments and IBM	1982	development of local network systems chips
Motorola and IBM	1982	370 microprocessor development and exchange of local network controller chip circuit design
Intel and IBM	1982	computer memory chip development
Motorola and National	1982	CMOS gateways
Motorola and Advanced Micro Devices	1982	256k RAM technology exchange
Microelectronics and Computer Technology Center[a]	1982	basic semiconductor research

[a]Eleven firms, including Control Data, Honeywell, Burroughs, Xerox, Intel, and MOSTEK.

acquired more than a dozen companies to support its integrated communications activities. Olivetti has been extremely active in acquiring small minority positions in niche-oriented companies, such as Docutel, Syntrex (word processing), Microoffice Systems Technology, Lanx (memory disks), Ithaca Intersystems (microcomputers), Stratus Computers, and Transaction Management (retail p.o.s systems).

Horizontal and Vertical Scope

Efforts to develop systems capability through agreements, acquisitions, and internal development are leading to a growing polarization of the information technology sector.

One set of firms is emerging that will focus on providing integrated information processing systems to end users. These firms will be capable of delivering systems that will include central and distributed data storage and processing, inter- and intrabuilding voice, video and data communications, and work station functions such as word processing and electronic mail. A second set of firms will focus on selling subsystems. These companies will provide one or more discrete products such as terminals, printers, personal computers, minicomputers, or PBX products to end users or intermediaries.

The horizontal scope of a firm's product offering is an increasingly important variable in this market. Many firms are attempting to increase the scope of their activities to participate in emerging systems markets in the areas of office automation, local networks, and integrated communication systems. The vertical scope of a firm's activities is also very important. It is possible to expand product lines without increasing the level of a firm's vertical integration. Within the set of firms attempting to develop systems capability, another type of polarization is developing between those firms that are vertically integrated and those that are not.

Non-integrated firms will rely on external suppliers for key components and subsystems. These suppliers may or may not also sell their products directly to end users. Japanese companies will be important suppliers to non-integrated systems companies. If Japanese firms eliminate other independent suppliers, sources of supply would become vulnerable as Japanese companies expand their marketing efforts to end users. Other suppliers such as Control Data, Storage Technology, and Qume also sell directly to end users as well as to OEM customers. Those systems companies that produce little or none of their own hardware will be dependent on such suppliers for technology and production. In the extreme case, where the systems supplier produces none of the hardware it

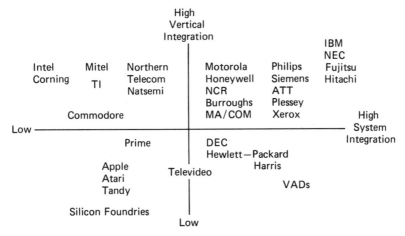

Figure 15 One strategic view of the information technology sector.

sells, the systems assembler becomes a value-added distributor. Value-added distributors, or systems houses, rely on software, service, and support capabilities to attract customers.

Participants in the information technology sector can be viewed in terms of their strategies on these two key dimensions. Their degree of systems emphasis and their level of vertical integration provide an important perspective on their chosen strategy. Figure 15 presents a number of leading firms on a map with these two dimensions.

Role of Value-Added Distributors

The potential role of value-added distributors (VAD's) raises several important issues. VADs may have an impact on the ongoing tension between systems and specialist suppliers. The development of VADs presents an opportunity to specialists. If such firms are successful as intermediaries between customers and producers, niche specialists could prosper at the expense of integrated systems suppliers.

Value-added distributors are expanding rapidly at the present time. These firms tend to specialize in very specific market niches, such as medical, insurance, accounting, hotel, or hardware store applications. Software and services designed specifically for a narrowly defined user segment are developed, and the distributor provides a high level of customization at the marketing and system design level.

The success of value-added distributors is particularly important to Japanese companies. These distributors provide the software, service, and support functions that are the greatest weaknesses of Japanese vendors. The potential combination of Japanese hardware and focused, customized VAD software and services poses a powerful force in the marketplace.

Three Market Approaches

Three primary marketing approaches will be competing in this sector. Although all three will continue to exist, it is likely that one form will dominate primary markets for information processing systems. The VAD or intermediary approach represents one potential market structure; the direct sales approach of the integrated systems suppliers represents another, and sales by specialist suppliers represents the third approach. Although it is difficult to assess which approach will predominate, some indications as to future trends can be seen now.

The components segment is again a good vehicle for assessing future trends in other sectors. An active components distribution industry has developed to serve as an intermediary between producers and users. These intermediaries offer superior service in terms of delivery time and a broad selection of products. Component distributors' sales have grown from $900 million in 1970 to about $5 billion in 1983. Their share of total electronics components sales has grown from 17.8% to 29% over that time period. Their growth appears to set a precedent for patterns in other industries, especially because service require-ments in this industry are much lower than in other segments. Independent distributors might be expected to be even more successful in industries where service needs are greater, if superior customer service is their distinc-tive competence.

This pattern is somewhat misleading, however. The independent component distributors exist at the discre-tion of their suppliers. Component producers value these distributors because they hold inventory, process paper, and handle logistics. Component producers sell direct to larger customers. In effect, distributors sell to secondary and tertiary customers, those 80% that account for 20% of sales. They hold inventory, often for older products, perform credit checking, and handle some of the less desirable aspects of the producer's business. When a distributor's customer gets big enough, the producer begins to sell direct, taking advantage of lower costs.

The Systems Market

A similar scenario could occur in the systems market. VADs can develop new markets, handle marginal accounts, hold inventory, take credit risks, and provide costly customized services. By developing customers and markets that would normally not be pursued by producers, they will contribute to market expansion and development. There is one major difference between the systems and components market, however. Important switching costs exist in the systems market. Intermediaries could build enduring relationships with users in the systems market.

Although intermediaries may be successful in many specialized market niches, it will be more difficult for them to pursue primary markets for information processing equipment. In such markets, the superior resources of the systems and specialist suppliers should predominate in the long run.

Specialist producers may also compete most effectively outside the mainstream. In primary systems markets, systems suppliers have several advantages over any set of specialist suppliers. Customers attempting to develop their own integrated system from a variety of sources face severe implementation problems. Compatibility is a key concern. Problems can be resolved, usually at some major expense, but the resulting system will be less efficient than a system that was designed to work as a system. Retrofitted systems sacrifice a great deal of efficiency. Support is also a key concern. Users that integrate their own systems must deal with a number of support and service organizations, none of whom wants responsibility for interface problems. Moreover, given current market trends, many of the diverse suppliers may opt to drop product lines or to postpone technical improvements. Some suppliers may go bankrupt; others will be acquired. Vendor relations will be very problematic. As a result, it is increasingly likely that customers will turn to systems suppliers. Their principal options are integrated suppliers or value-added distributors. I believe customers in the mainstream of the market will turn to integrated suppliers most frequently. When the full service capabilities of a systems supplier are offered to an end user, the one advantage of the value-added distributor is neutralized.

Japanese suppliers seem to appreciate this likelihood. Although they are actively cultivating relationships with value-added distributors, the primary thrusts of the leading companies are toward direct distribution activities. This pattern is already seen in Japanese activities in the U.S. market.

The leading Japanese firms possess excellent potential systems capabilities. Each of the six leading companies is active in a wide range of information technology markets. NEC, Fujitsu, and Hitachi in particular operate in virtually all segments of the market. Although they now make

extensive use of OEM and VAD agreements, they will ultimately emerge as vertically integrated, systems-oriented
suppliers. Japanese activities in the U.S. market will follow
a predictable pattern. Initial activities in the U.S. market
have focused on individual market niches, such as
components, printers, and CPUs. These products were
exported from Japan and sold through independent
distributors or to OEM customers. Over time, however,
the level of Japanese involvement in distribution activities
has tended to increase. In several cases, independent
marketing agents have been replaced with direct sales
forces managed through joint ventures. In the mainframe
market, Fujitsu has expanded its activities in this way,
first by acquiring a minority interest in Amdahl, and second
by taking a majority ownership position in a joint venture
with TRW. Fujitsu acquired full ownership of this joint
venture in 1983.

Japanese Manufacturing Activities in the United States

At the same time that Japanese participation in the U.S.
marketing channel is increasing, they have also tended to
expand their U.S. manufacturing activities. The most
highly evolved example of this approach is again the semiconductor industry. Each of the six leading Japanese firms
operates a wholly owned affiliate in this market in the
United States. Each of these affiliates manufactures semiconductor memory and other products in the United States.
All of these affiliates were built, not acquired.

I believe Japanese activities in other market segments
will follow this pattern. Japanese firms will not expand
primarily through acquisitions of existing U.S. companies. They will establish and develop their own wholly
owned affiliates to engage in direct distribution and grow-

ing assembly and manufacturing activity. As seen in Figure 16, their operations will migrate from the upper left to the lower right as they expand activity in a given segment.

There are several reasons to expect this pattern. My discussions with Japanese managers suggest that many Japanese firms have not had good experiences with U.S. agreements and acquisitions. There has been a very high

Table 27   Activities of Leading Japanese Firms in Information Technology Markets

Product	Firm					
	NEC	Fujitsu	Hitachi	Toshiba	Oki	Mitsubishi
Semiconductors						
Memories	x	x	x	x	x	x
VLSI logic micro-processors	x	x	x	x	x	x
Passive components	x	x	x	x	x	x
Disk drives	x	x	x			x
Printers	x	x	x	x	x	
Terminals	x	x	x			
Modems	x	x	x			
Facsimile	x	x	x	x	x	x
Word processors	x	x	x	x		
Personal computers	x	x	x	x	x	
Minicomputers	x	x	x	x	x	x
Small business systems	x	x	x	x	x	x
Mainframes	x	x	x			
PBX	x	x	x	x	x	
Switching systems	x	x	x			
Software	x	x	x		x	

level of antagonism in some existing agreements and acquisitions in the United States. Ricoh was involved in difficult litigation for years in its attempt to terminate its distribution agreements with Savin Corporation.[7] Fujitsu experienced some significant problems in its negotiations with TRW. According to private sources, Fujitsu's CEO insisted in these negotiations that the joint venture's products bear the FACOM brand name. Despite Fujitsu's majority ownership position, the company's products carried the TFC (TRW-Fujitsu Corporation) label. Given these and other experiences that have been widely publicized in Japan, many companies have avoided further agreements and acquisitions. For example, Fujitsu expressed no interest in Memorex when it put itself on the acquisition block, even though Fujitsu had a long-standing OEM supply agreement with the company.

Most Japanese firms vastly prefer to start with a virgin work force that can be trained and socialized in the company way. They do not wish to attempt to integrate existing personnel, systems, and management into their own organizations. The "green fields" approach has been followed by Sony, Honda, Nissan, Kikkoman, and other successful Japanese investors in the United States.

There is also the question of government approval. Such approval is unlikely to be immediately forthcoming for any major acquisitions. Even the recent GM–Toyota agreement, which took extensive pressure and significant concessions to realize, faces a tough and probably lengthy review by the Federal Trade Commission. The FTC's favorable review of IBM's investment in Intel, by comparison, took less than three weeks.

THE AUSTRALIAN EXPERIMENT

Predictions about Japan's activities in the U.S. market are supported by observing Japanese activities in Australia.

Manufacturing	Marketing				
	Third Party		Equity Ties		
			Joint Ventures		
	Independent Agents	OEM Agreements	Minority	Majority	Wholly Owned
	Personal Computers				
Japan Only	Oki	NEC*			
			Mainframes		
U. S. Assembly		NASCO	Amdahl	TRW–Fujitsu	
U. S. Manufacturing					**Semiconductors** Oki Toshiba Fujitsu NEC Hitachi Mitsubishi

Figure 16 Marketing and manufacturing strategies for Japanese companies, by segment.
*NEC uses a hybrid distribution system, selling through its wholly owned NEC Electronics as well as through independent distributors.

The country offers an ideal test market for Japanese computer companies. It is an extremely open market with easy access; it is an English language market. Public agencies have purchased information processing equipment on a strict low-bid basis. Virtually every major vendor is active in Australia. In short, it provides an excellent location for launching an initial marketing effort; for learning, experimentation, and refinement of strategies prior to entering other markets. Japanese activities in this market will provide insights into their future activities in other markets.

Several immediate observations about Japanese activities in the Australian information processing market can be made. There is virtually no overlap of Japanese activities in Australia. Fujitsu alone is active in the mainframe market. Mitsubishi is active in the small business systems market, and NEC is the Japanese leader in the personal computer market. This pattern of limited overlap appears in other Asian markets as well.[8] The distribution approach used in Australia is also interesting. Fujitsu, the primary Japanese force in Australia, relies almost entirely on a direct sales force.[9] Its affiliate, FACOM Australia, is a wholly owned affiliate.

The history of FACOM Australia provides some insights into Fujitsu's approach to information processing markets. FACOM Australia has served as a test market and a training ground for managers. FACOM's former head of marketing is now head of marketing in the United States. FACOM Australia was founded in 1972 and initially managed by a team of Japanese expatriates. This management team was replaced by a team of Australian managers in 1976, who were hired from leading Australian computer companies, primarily IBM Australia Ltd. FACOM's results showed immediate improvement. From a market share of under 1% in 1976, its share rose to 5% in 1980 and almost 10% in 1982.

FACOM's sales are primarily in its large M-series systems. These are large systems; the average price for a M-200 system is over $3 million. Over 120 M-series systems have been sold in Australia, which accounts for more than three-quarters of all Fujitsu installations outside of Japan. Fujitsu also sells its V-series medium-range and small business systems in Australia, but less than 100 of these smaller systems have been sold. The focus of their efforts in Australia has been on high-end systems sold through a direct sales force.

It is notable that Fujitsu competes against Amdahl and ICL in Australia. Amdahl's systems are also produced by

Fujitsu, and ICL's will carry increasing Fujitsu content, so any competition between these companies seems unjustifiable. This problem is minimized by several arrangements. First, Amdahl and FACOM share service and administrative overheads in Australia. Second, the IBM-compatible market is reserved for Amdahl. Third, ICL's sales and administrative activities appear to be moving under FACOM's umbrella, and there is an informal agreement that ICL and FACOM will not "sell against" each other. Although significant conflicts do occur in the field as these three organizations attempt to market their systems, this approach is useful for projecting what may evolve in the United States and elsewhere.

FACOM's market share performance has been the greatest Japanese success in foreign information processing markets. The reasons for that success are not very subtle. Fujitsu has been willing to invest heavily and incur ongoing losses in Australia. FACOM reported a loss of over $5 million for its 1982 fiscal year, bringing the total investment in Australia to over $50 million. Fujitsu has yet to realize any positive financial returns from its activities in Australia. The following example illustrates why.

Churchill Company Ltd.

The Churchill Company publicized its intentions to buy two mainframes in the two-MIPS (million instructions per second) range. Informal bids were tendered by a number of vendors, but four were encouraged to continue their efforts. The four, with starting "bids," were:

Vendor	System	MIPS	Price (million)
IBM	two 3033Ns	4.5	$5.5
FACOM	one M180 and one M200	5.0	$4.5
NASCO	two AS7000	3.1	$2.5
Amdahl	two V7Bs	3.1	$2.4

After further discussion, the competition was reduced to IBM and FACOM. IBM offered two 3033 systems with a total of three MIPS for $4 million; FACOM offered two M180 systems with three MIPS for $2.4 million, plus a $400,000 allowance for the trade-in of an obsolete older system and a free conversion of the computers' operating system to IBM compatibility. The conversion was valued at $200,000 or more. The FACOM package cost less than half of the IBM package.

The end result in the Churchill Company's case was the purchase of two M180 systems for a total of $1.6 million less a $400,000 trade allowance, and a free operating system conversion. FACOM's offer was approximately one-fourth the cost of an IBM system with equivalent data processing capacity. Such tactics have been the source of FACOM's market share growth in Australia.

If the Australian market provides insights into future Japanese activities, it also offers insight into the implications of increased Japanese activity in world markets. The share of market held by all Japanese companies in the Australian data processing industry has increased from 2 to 14% in the last five years. How has this increase affected others in the market?

The most important observation is that it has not appeared to affect IBM adversely at all. IBM's market share in Australia has actually increased over the last three years. FACOM has taken sites away from IBM, but IBM has also become increasingly aggressive. The result is that everyone else in the market has lost share. Burroughs, Univac, NCR, Control Data, and Honeywell as a group have lost net market share of 6.2% in the last three years alone. The leading Australian computer maker, Hartley Ltd., went bankrupt in 1982.

PROBABLE WORLD SCENARIO

These events point to a probable scenario for other world information technology markets. Secondary producers will find themselves squeezed harder and harder by aggressive Japanese competitors and a revitalized IBM. In the mainframe systems market, the total market share held by Japanese suppliers and IBM will expand by as much as 10% in this decade. A similar scenario will be played out in other segments. A few dominant firms will increase their share as a group at the expense of smaller companies.

Consolidation of market shares in individual product and geographic market segments is the first round in a broader consolidation of world data processing markets. Dominant firms in each segment will later find themselves competing primarily against dominant firms from other segments, as they expand their activities to new markets. A second round of consolidation will create a few giant companies with resources and capabilities in almost all major segments of the information technology sector.

This scenario suggests that the secondary firms in this industry will find it increasingly difficult to compete with the leading companies. To an extent, I believe that will be true. This process will be buffered by the successful segmentation efforts of secondary firms and new entrants. There will be niches in which smaller or slower companies can survive, but not many. Segments with high profit potential will attract the attention of both the larger established companies and new ventures. There are some defensible segments in this industry, or markets in which specialists can build barriers to entry. Such segments must exhibit a unique user base and a unique and superior technology base. Firms in such positions will survive and prosper. Firms operating in the open field will not unless they have superior resources or responsiveness to market and technology opportunities.

Table 28   Australian Market Share Trends, Hardware
Only (1980–1982)

	Share of Hardware Market by Value		
Company	1980	1981	1982
IBM	33.9%	32.9%	34.4%
Honeywell	12.1	11.4	10.5
FACOM	5.4	7.9	9.3
Burroughs	10.5	8.8	8.1
ICL	8.5	8.4	7.4
Univac	8.3	7.2	6.8
CDC	5.7	5.6	5.2
DEC	4.4	4.7	4.6
NCR	3.8	3.8	3.6
Datapoint	0.0	1.7	1.5
NASCO	0.0	0.9	1.3
HP	0.0	1.2	1.3
Prime	0.0	1.1	1.2
Amdahl	1.1	0.8	0.9
DG	0.0	0.85	0.8
Wang	0.0	0.65	0.6

SOURCE: Australasian Computerworld.

Although the end result will vary by segment, there are three possible outcomes. A segment could become dominated by a niche specialist. Such segments must display unique user and technology bases if the specialists are to resist inroads by large full-line companies. Specialists can compete most effectively where there is no linkage to a larger system, and where there are unique needs and technology conditions. Segments dominated by the integrated systems suppliers will exhibit relatively common user characteristics and the market will be served by technology from the mainstream of systems development. In some cases, specialists and system suppliers could coexist, but that would represent an unstable condition.

The word processing market provides an example. It is extremely unlikely that producers specializing in discrete word processors will flourish. Word processing has become a mainstream market, and it is served by personal computers and work station suppliers. For only a small additional cost (and in some cases for a lower cost) a machine with many more functions can be purchased instead of a word processor. Taking this example one step further, a stand-alone personal computer can be superceded by a networked microcomputer, terminal or work station. If public networks or common carriers are available, niche products can plug in to existing systems, but the product must incorporate an increasing range of functions and capabilities to compete in this way.

The internalization of many functions is already occurring. The next phase is beginning to be enacted. The office systems market provides an example. There are many possible ways in which this market can be served. A user with extensive central processing activities could purchase a DEC minicomputer with a set of terminals, or if significant work station activity is also needed, a set of Rainbow or DECMATE personal computers. An alternative would be to use a set of Lisa work stations connected to an Ethernet network. Such an approach would be better suited to users with no central data processing or storage needs and extensive, sophisticated work station requirements. Other users might prefer an American Bell or other PBX-based system with sophisticated and extensive communications capabilities, but more limited central processing and work station functions. The needs of individual customers will lead them to prefer one type of system over another, but each type is capable of serving mainstream users. Over time, the overlap across these types of systems will increase as each set of companies expands its activities.

It is impossible to predict which approach will prevail, but it is likely that one approach will dominate the mainstream, and it is also likely that more and more users will fall into the category of mainstream users over time. This will occur as more functions and options are added to existing systems and as technical standards begin to converge and integrate. For example, the IBM PC is not currently used to support CAD/CAM activities. A CAD/CAM package was recently announced for the PC, however, and given its ability to attach to larger IBM computers, it will begin to appear in that user segment. The Apple II is experiencing a similar expansion of applications. However, these products must compete against specialized work stations designed for specific use in individual segments.

No single approach can do everything better than others, and there will be areas where specialists thrive. There is still plenty of opportunity for new entrants in this industry, but ultimately a consolidation of approaches and competitors can be expected. The result could be an industry structure which is increasingly dominated by large firms active in a range of segments. This category of firms will include the major Japanese suppliers, ATT, IBM, Xerox, Philips, Siemens, and the emerging French representative, for starters. A second set of firms in this category will include Wang, Motorola, Olivetti, Honeywell, DEC, Hewlett-Packard, and Plessey.

The first and most obvious distinction that will separate the winners from the losers in this industry over the next decade is their degree of international activity. Global firms will dominate virtually every market segment. It will be virtually impossible to be competitive in this industry without a large foreign sales base. A second distinction is likely to be the degree of vertical integration in key component areas. Only firms with semiconductor operations at or above minimum-efficient-scale levels are likely to prosper in this industry. This base is necessary to ensure the availability of key components, to achieve cost efficiency, and to ensure state-of-the-art technology. There are alternative means of achieving these benefits, but they require efforts and agreements that at best approximate a vertical integration strategy.

The foreseeable future of this sector will involve tremendous chaos. It is difficult to ascertain the speed and direction of the market. Competitors of every shape and size are lining up at the starting line. All want to gain a part of this most promising of all industries. The course will be complex, the competition will be fierce, and the pace will be frantic. More firms will lose than win. There are presently almost 200 producers of personal computers in the United States. How many will there be in 1990? For most of those firms that survive the race in this and other segments, the second leg of the race posts them against the winners from other segments.

The real prize in this race is leadership in the marketplace. Only a few rivals can even think of achieving leadership across this broadening sector. IBM and ATT can realistically aim for this goal. The French will endeavor to achieve a measure of leadership in this sector, but the Japanese industry is the only other real contender. The ultimate confrontation in this sector pits IBM and ATT against the Japanese. That confrontation is at least 10 years away. The skirmishing going on today is only a warm-up for the real event. In the interim, technical standards and market structures will converge and consolidate.

The race between the United States and Japan in this sector is perhaps the most important ongoing event in the world today. It is perhaps more important than the arms race in determining the future of world societies. The outcome of this race will affect how almost all people live and work on a daily basis. The future of the world economic order rests on its outcome. That is also true in the arms race, but there is one important difference:

*Greater speed and intensity in the race for leader-
ship in the information technology sector can only
benefit mankind.*

Japanese activities in any market have always led to
improvements in product quality and value, service and
product design. Their cost reduction efforts have lowered
prices, raised demand, and increased consumer benefits.
Japanese industry is the most powerful force for industrial progress in the world today. Their efforts in the information technology sector will lead to those same benefits
in this market and speed the adoption of productivity-
and life-enhancing technologies. Just as society would
benefit from a deceleration in the arms race, society will
benefit from acceleration of this race.

The race for leadership in the information technology
sector is not a zero-sum game. Opportunities for mutual
advancement exist in this industry. Costs can be shared,
for example, but the best opportunity for mutual progress
comes from clean competition. If the honest efforts and
successes of one party push others on to greater achievements, society will benefit most. The pace and intensity
of the race are very telling on the participants, but it is in
the public interest to force the pace of progress.

The issue that remains is how to ensure honest, fair,
and durable standards of conduct in this industry. Ques-
tionable commercial, legal or political actions can only
damage the integrity of the race. Public policies and international agreements designed to limit such activities must
be enforced. Perhaps more important, international
agreements governing public protection and promotion of
domestic industries must be pushed forward.

The distinction between public and private participants
in this sector will of course continue to shrink over time.
Public support in many forms will be the rule in all coun-

tries. If public support becomes too intense, however, there is the risk of all-out commercial warfare. Any all-out commercial warfare would inevitably result in global fragmentation of the market, which would reduce efficiency and the speed of market development. It would of course increase global tension, hinder growth and development, and destroy common paths of progress. That would be a tragedy in an industry which holds a unique potential for bringing the world closer together.

There are indications that positive relations and understandings are being built. Many cooperative agreements have been signed between Japanese and U.S. parties in the last year. NTT and ATT have initiated a technology exchange agreement. IBM has initiated agreements with Matsushita, Japan's leading consumer electronics company and Orient Leasing, the larget leasing company in Japan.[10] A high-technology accord was signed by U.S. and Japanese government officials in 1982[11]. The prospect for further cooperation between U.S. and Japanese firms and governments in this industry is very good at this time. The terms have yet to be determined, but the resolve for mutual cooperation appears strong.

The spirit of cooperation is essential, but it must not detract from the main objective. The information technology sector is today what North America was 200 years ago—a large undeveloped area with limitless potential. Many nations attempted to secure all or part of the continent—England, France, Spain, Russia, and the fledgling United States. Only one participant had the vision to view the development of the bulk of the continent as its manifest destiny. Bold, visionary leaders exist today in the information technology sector. Their efforts will appear heroic to future generations, but the scale of their activities will be dwarfed by the realities of the sector in years to come.

REFERENCES AND NOTES

1. "A Capital Crunch That Could Change An Industry," *Business Week*, March 23, 1981, p. 82–84.

2. "International Competition in Advanced Industrial Sectors." A Report prepared for the Joint Economic Committee, Congress of the United States (Washington: Government Prnting Office, 1982) pp. 40–41.

3. *Wall Street Journal*, July 22, 1982, p. 3.

4. "Unit of ATT, N. V. Philips Set Joint Venture," *Wall Street Journal*, January 6, 1983, p. 2.

5. *Business Week*, October 4, 1982, p. 86.

6. "Wang Signs Technology Pact With California Company," Boston Globe, October 29, 1981, p. 47.

7. "Savin Sues," *Wall Street Journal*, May 13, 1977, p. 20; "Savin Seeks to End Tie With (Ricoh)," *Wall Street Journal*, October 3, 1977, p. 14; "Savin Agrees to Settle Dispute With Ricoh," *Wall Street Journal*, February 22, 1978, p. 10.

8. "Japan's Lone-wolf Tactics in Computers," *Business Week*, September 21, 1981, p. 50.

9. Virtually all of Fujitsu's sales people in Australia are hired as independent contractors because of employee tax benefits, but they function as a captive sales force. This approach also contributes to the growth of value-added distributors, as sales contractors can also contract to customers for service and installation agreements independent of FACOM.

10. "IBM Abandons Its Go-it-alone Stance," *Business Week*, March 14, 1983, p. 41; *Wall Street Journal*, March 17, 1983, p. 16; *Electronic News*, March 21, 1983, p. 24. Another possible agreement has been discussed with Mitsubishi. See: "Mitsubishi and IBM May Tie in Computer Field," *Japan Economic Journal*, February 4, 1983, p. 3.

11. Some of the recent cooperative agreements and discussions between the U. S. and Japanese public sectors are described in: "Military Technology Swap," *Japan Economic Journal*, January 25, 1983, p. 4; "Technology (Cooperation) Meeting Ends," *Mainichi Daily News*, August 8, 1982,

p. 5. The second article states "the Japan–U.S. high technology working group, formed earlier in the year," held its first formal meeting in Hawaii in July. A second "informal but productive consultation on expansion of high technology cooperation and promotion of research and development" was held in August. Formal meetings were also held in September and October of 1982. These meetings led to a bilateral high-technology agreement. See "U.S., Japan Downplaying New High-Tech Accord," *Electronic News*, November 8, 1982, p. 39.

Index

265